Ph ... the world

A UNESCO survey

ROGER-POL DROIT

Philosophy and democracy in the world

A UNESCO survey
Foreword by Federico Mayor

Translation by Catherine Cullen

UNESCO PUBLISHING

The authors are responsible for the choice and presentation of the facts contained in this book as well as for the opinions expressed, which are not necessarily those of UNESCO and do not commit the Organization.

CONTENTS

PART THREE
WHAT CAN BE DONE?

ANNEXES

A SCHOOL FOR FREEDOM

As you who have just opened this book already know, we are living in a period which, more than any other, is a time of great dangers and great hopes. Whether you live in the North or the South, whether you are young or old, you know that we are, all of us together, confronted by major planetary risks in a number of basic areas. Never has humanity held such means of destruction, and never has it had at its disposal such means of construction. This is why we encounter new difficulties every day, and see new initiatives aimed at making the world a more human place.

In this time of change, does philosophy have a role to play? The answer is, resoundingly, yes. I believe the contribution of philosophers to be essential for understanding our present and building the societies of tomorrow. That is why I have decided to see to it personally that UNESCO will develop its activities in the area of philosophy. There are two main reasons for this conviction, which I would like to explain briefly.

First of all, the vast heritage of world philosophy provides a number of intellectual tools which can help us to better understand the changes taking place before our eyes. This of course does not mean we can simply turn to past or present philosophers for ready-made answers. Nevertheless, it is important to consult this extraordinary stock of ideas and concepts offered by philosophical doctrines. Tools can be found there to help us develop the new analyses we need. It should not be forgotten that in all cultures the oldest and deepest source of interdisciplinary thinking stems from the philosophers. For them, the need to remove the barriers around fields of knowledge, to compare different theoretical approaches, to broaden as far as possible the scope of thought, is no recent requirement, it is the natural horizon of their spiritual quest.

In this sense, philosophy is a school for freedom. It encourages the constant renewal of thought. Its remedy against intellectual routine is the creation of new concepts. *"Dare to have new ideas! Ideas that no one has ever had before."*

That is the main thrust of philosophy. It is why we must invite philosophers to analyze the major problems facing humanity today, in all areas. UNESCO's mission is not to compete with the many research institutions throughout the world pursuing specialized studies in, for example, the history of philosophy or the scholarly analysis of philosophical doctrine. Its task is different; it is to incite philosophers to participate actively in international thinking on the world's problems, through writing, public meetings, recorded interviews and media-related action.

Judging for oneself

The second reason why I believe that philosophy is crucial to the building of our future is doubtless even more compelling. It concerns education. The widely diffused, accessible and relevant teaching of philosophy contributes in an essential way to the development of free citizens. It encourages one to judge for oneself, to confront all sorts of arguments, to respect what others have to say, and to submit only to the authority of reason. In this way, too, it is undeniably a school for freedom.

This practical training in basic rights also leads to the discovery of the universal. It enlarges our capacity for reflection, and the scope of our thinking, by helping us to understand unaccustomed points of view. It allows us to comprehend, beyond the diversity of the answers, the degree to which the basic questions of life actually make humans look more alike rather than more different from one another. For example, the questions about the foundations of knowledge, the values that should guide our acts, the respect for others, and our responsability towards future generations, are truly universal.

Such an initiation to philosophical reflection, open and accessible to all, is a concrete embodiment of the "society of minds" that Paul Valéry called for in the thirties, in the context of the Office of International Intellectual Cooperation. In this sense, everything that enhances possibilities for teaching philosophy contributes to building "defences of peace in the minds of men", one of UNESCO's founding tasks. This organization has thus always had as a mission to support the development of philosophy teaching to the young as well as to adults. For this support to be effective, for UNESCO's initiatives to catalyze energies, precise knowledge of the situation of philosophy teaching around the world is indispensable.

Since its creation, UNESCO has taken various steps towards this goal: in 1950, the General Conference during its fifth session decided to organize "an inquiry into the place occupied by the teaching of philosophy in the different educational systems, the way it is taught and its influence on the training of the citizen" (resolution n° 4-1212). This first survey, whose results were published by UNESCO in 1953 under the direction of the French philosopher Georges Canguilhem, needed to be updated, expanded, and systematized. That is the goal of the programme "Philosophy and democracy in the world" which I have placed under the responsability of the philosopher and journalist Roger-Pol Droit.

New Democracies

Between the middle of the twentieth century and its close, there have been major political and cultural transformations. In a way, we no longer live on quite the same planet as the men and women of the 1950's. Philosophy and its teaching have doubtless also changed. But above all, new forms of democratic life have arisen in Africa, in Asia, in post-communist Europe, in a Latin America freeing itself from military dictatorships, and in certain

Arab countries. Furthermore, in the course of this half-century, UNESCO has also been transformed. It has seen a considerable increase in the number of Member States and in the scope of its activities. After weathering a number of crises, it has been able to renew itself and come back to its founding principles.

A few figures will give an idea of the difference between the enquiry of 1951 and today's survey. The first only really involved, in the last analysis, nine countries. The data collected by the programme "Philosophy and democracy in the world" come from 66 countries, whose multiple responses have been gathered and tabulated in just a few months. Independently of the quantitative aspect, unprecedented in this area, the survey has produced four major findings, and a very useful sketch of the preliminary analyses.

The report by Roger-Pol Droit also assembles an important series of concrete proposals concerning, for example, a multi-level pedagogical approach associating books, distance teaching, audiovisual and computer technologies. This concrete aspect is essential, since any changes, albeit minimal, which an effort of this type can produce are to my mind major victories over universal bureaucracy. There are so many meetings, colloquia, seminars, and expert commissions that yield no practical proposals at all! The mere fact that the proposals here are so numerous and detailed augurs well for their concrete realization.

What exactly are the links between philosophy and democracy? I think a crucial point should be emphasized right now, in advance of the analyses and conclusions of this book. We have observed that the teaching of philosophy develops and spreads concomitantly with democracy. Dictatorships and totalitarian systems forbid it or pervert it from its vocation as a force for freedom. The Paris declaration for philosophy adopted by the participants during the International Study Days of "Philosophy and democracy in the world" organized by UNESCO on the 15th and 16th of February, 1995, rightly emphasizes that "philosophy education, by training independently-minded, thoughtful people, capable of resisting various forms of propaganda, fanaticism, exclusion and intolerance, contributes to peace and prepares everyone to shoulder their responsibilities in regard to the great questions of the contemporary world, particularly in the field of ethics." This important text, which deserves to be widely distributed, also recalls, quite appropriately, that "the development of philosophical reflection, in education and in cultural life, makes a major contribution to the training of citizens, by exercizing their capacity for judgement, which is fundamental in any democracy."

The autonomy of philosophy

I wish, here, to forestall a possible confusion. It would be a mistake to see philosophy and democracy as totally equivalent. It would be wrong to believe that philosophy is necessarily, and by its very nature, on the side of democracy. We would be victims of an illusion if we wanted to develop the teaching of philosophy from a conviction that it would serve, automatically and conveniently, the diffusion of democratic values. While there is a fundamental relation between philosophy's freedom of thought and speech, on the one hand, and the equality and pluralism characteristic of democracy, on the other, it cannot be inferred from this that all philosophers are of necessity democratic.

History provides numerous examples of the close links between philosophical reflection and democracy. For example, Athens in the fifth century B.C., France in the eighteenth century, Western Europe in 1848, Eastern Europe since 1989. However, throughout history, there have been great philosophers who were not politically what we would call democrats. Does this mean that we should omit Plato, Nietzsche, or Heidegger from the study of philosophy? That would be absurd. We should rather conclude that philosophy is autonomous. As a school for freedom, it cannot be forced to support any political regime or ideology. It endlessly submits everything to critical scrutiny, including its own existence, and its methods.

It is no doubt this that makes philosophy most similar to democracy: they have the same capacity for self-criticism.

Philosophy continuously questions itself. It believes in the fecundity of doubt. This is not so with dogma. Democracy also questions itself, not hesitating to underline its own weaknesses, as is obviously not the case with dictatorships and totalitarianisms. The link between philosophy and democracy is, then, not on the surface, in the play of opinions and the multiplicity of dissonant speech. It lies in the basic fact that both encourage criticism that respects the dignity of others. They urge each of us to exercise our capacity for judgement, to choose for ourselves the best form of political and social organization, to find our own values, in short, to become fully what each of us is, a free being. Among so many dangers, we have no other hope.

Federico MAYOR
Director-General of UNESCO

CONSTITUTION OF THE UNITED NATIONS
EDUCATIONAL, SCIENTIFIC AND CULTURAL ORGANIZATION (Extracts)

Adopted in London on 16 November 1945.

Preamble

The Governments of the States Parties to this Constitution on behalf of their peoples declare:

That since wars begin in the minds of men, it is in the minds of men that the defences of peace must be constructed;

That ignorance of each other's ways and lives has been a common cause, throughout the history of mankind, of that suspicion and mistrust between the peoples of the world through which their differences have all too often broken into war;

That the great and terrible war which has now ended was a war made possible by the denial of the democratic principles of the dignity, equality and mutual respect of men, and by the propagation, in their place, through ignorance and prejudice, of the doctrine of the inequality of men and races;

That the wide diffusion of culture, and the education of humanity for justice and liberty and peace are indispensable to the dignity of man and constitute a sacred duty which all the nations must fulfil in a spirit of mutual assistance and concern;

That a peace based exclusively upon the political and economic arrangements of governments would not be a peace which could secure the unanimous, lasting and sincere support of the peoples of the world, and that the peace must therefore be founded, if it is not to fail, upon the intellectual and moral solidarity of mankind.

For these reasons, the States Parties to this Constitution, believing in full and equal opportunities for education for all, in the unrestricted pursuit of objective truth, and in the free exchange of ideas and knowledge, are agreed and determined to develop and to increase the means of communication between their peoples and to employ these means for the purposes of mutual understanding and a truer and more perfect knowledge of each other's lives;

In consequence whereof they do hereby create the United Nations Educational, Scientific and Cultural Organization for the purpose of advancing, through the education and scientific and cultural relations of the peoples of the world, the objectives of international peace and of the common welfare of mankind for which the United Nations Organization was established and which its Charter proclaims.

Article I. Purposes and functions

1. The purpose of the Organization is to contribute to peace and security by promoting collaboration among the nations through education, science and culture in order to further universal respect for justice, for the rule of law and for the human rights and fundamental freedoms which are affirmed for the peoples of the world, without distinction of race, sex, language or religion, by the Charter of the United Nations.

2. To realize this purpose the Organization will:

(a) Collaborate in the work of advancing the mutual knowledge and understanding of peoples, through all means of mass communication and to that end recommend such international agreements as may be necessary to promote the free flow of ideas by word and image;

(b) Give fresh impulse to popular education and to the spread of culture:
By collaborating with Members, at their request, in the development of educational activities;
By instituting collaboration among the nations to advance the ideal of equality of educational opportunity without regard to race, sex or any distinctions, economic or social;
By suggesting educational methods best suited to prepare the children of the world for the responsibilities of freedom;

(c) Maintain, increase and diffuse knowledge:
By assuring the conservation and protection of the world's inheritance of books, works of art and monuments of history and science, and recommending to the nations concerned the necessary international conventions;
By encouraging co-operation among the nations in all branches of intellectual activity, including the international exchange of persons active in the fields of education, science and culture and the exchange of publications, objects of artistic and scientific interest and other materials of information.

We, the participants in the International Study Days on "Philosophy and Democracy in the World" organized by UNESCO in Paris on 15 and 16 February 1995,

Note that the problems with which philosophy deals are the universal problems of human life and existence;

Believe that philosophical reflection can and should contribute to the understanding and conduct of human affairs;

Consider that the practice of philosophy, which does not exclude any idea from free discussion and which endeavors to establish the exact definition of concepts used, to verify the validity of lines of reasoning and to scrutinize closely the arguments of others, enables each individual to learn to think independ-ently;

Emphasize that philosophy teaching encourages open-mindedness, civic responsibility, understanding and tolerance among individuals and groups;

Reaffirm that philosophy education, by training independ-ently-minded, thoughtful people, capable of resisting various forms of propaganda, prepares everyone to shoulder their responsibilities in regard to the great questions of the contemporary world, particularly in the field of ethics;

Confirm that the development of philosophical debate in education and in cultural life makes a major contribution to the training of citizens, by exercising their capacity for judgment, which is fundamental in any democracy.

Committing ourselves to do everything in our power in our institutions and in our respective countries to achieve these objectives, we therefore declare that:

All individuals everywhere should be entitled to engage in the free pursuit of philosophy in all its forms and all places where it may be practiced;

Philosophy teaching should be maintained or expanded where it exists, introduced where it does not yet exist, and designated explicitly as «philosophy»;

Philosophy teaching should be provided by qualified teachers, specially trained for that purpose, and should not be subordinated to any overriding economic, technical, religious, political or ideological requirements;

While remaining independent, philosophy teaching should wherever possible be effectively linked to academic or vocational training in all fields;

The distribution of books which are accessible both in language and in sales price to a wide readership, the production of radio and television programs, audio and video-cassettes, the use for educational purposes of all forms of audio-visual and informational technology, the creation of multiple opportunities for free discussion, and all types of initiative likely to provide the largest possible number of people with a grounding in philosophical issues and methods should be encouraged with a view to providing philosophy education for adults;

Knowledge of philosophical insight in different cultures, comparison of what each has to offer, analyses of what brings them closer together and what separates them, should be pursued and supported by research and teaching institutions;

Philosophy as the free pursuit of inquiry, cannot consider any truth to be final, and encourages respect for the convictions of the individual but should in no circumstances, at the risk of denying its own nature, accept doctrines which deny the liberty of others, affront human dignity and sow the seeds of barbarity.

This declaration was adopted by:

Pr Ruben G. Apressian (Moscow Academy of Sciences Institute of Philosophy, Russian Federation), Pr Tanella Boni-Kone (University of Abidjan, Cote d'Ivoire), Pr Tzotcho Boyadjiev (University of Saint Clement Ohrid, Sofia, Bulgaria), Pr In-Suk Cha (Secretary General of the National Commission for UNESCO of the Republic of Korea, Seoul, Republic of Korea), Pr Marilena Chaui (University of Sao Paulo, Brazil), Pr Donald Davidson (University of Berkeley, USA), Pr Souleymane Bachir Diagne (University of Dakar, Senegal), Pr Francois Dossou (National University of Benin, Cotonou, Benin), Pr Michael Dummett (Oxford, United Kingdom), Pr Artan Fuga (University of Tirana, Albania), Pr Humberto Giannini (University of Santiago de Chile, Chile), Pr Paulin J. Hountondji (National University of Benin, Cotonou, Benin), Pr Ioanna Kuçuradi (Secretary General of the International Federation of the Societies of Philosophy, Ankara, Turkey), Pr Dominique Lecourt (University of Paris VII, Paris, France), Pr Nelly Motroshilova (University of Moscow, Russian Federation), Pr Satchidananda Murty (Vice-president of the International Federation of the Societies of Philosophy, India), Pr Ulrich Johannes Schneider (University of Leipzig, Germany), Pr Peter Serracino Inglott (Rector of the University of Malta), H.E. Mohammed Allal Sinaceur (Former Director of the Division of Philosophy of UNESCO, Rabat, Morocco), Pr Richard Shusterman (Temple University, Philadelphia, USA), Pr Fathi Triki (Dean of the Faculty of Literature and Social Sciences of Sfax, Tunisia), Pr Susana Villavicencio (University of Buenos Aires, Argentina).

INTRODUCTORY NOTE

The following pages present questions, information, viewpoints, hypotheses, and proposals. They do not provide definitive answers.

Their aim is to open up a new field of reflection and debate on the place of philosophy in today's cultures, and on the development of citizens' capacities for independent judgement.

These first elements of data and analyses are placed at the disposal of those who will want to pursue this open approach, complete it, or transform it, according to their own viewpoints.

This book is therefore an incentive, not a conclusion.

As a temporary synthesis, it tries to be as clear and accessible as possible.

It is not a detailed study of all the specific cases.

To dispel any misunderstandings, four features of this book should be clarified, once and for all.

1– It deals with only one subject: the problems raised by the link between philosophical education and democratic processes in the contemporary world. It is not an exhaustive description of the organization of philosophy teaching in all countries. Nor is it a summary of the state of philosophy, describing its present development, theoretical tendencies, current trends, etc.

2 – On this single subject, it puts into perspective new data from 66 countries, collected in less than a year by the UNESCO Division of Philosophy. There are more than 2000 pages of documentation, so their detailed analysis could only be summarized.

3 – The report is completed by extracts from several studies especially commissioned for UNESCO and by other, mostly unpublished documents. Some of these "references" have been intentionally appended to the main text, so as to allow readers to choose their own path and interpretations.

4 – The author believes that he should not conceal his own opinions or conclusions, but that at the same time he must allow the reader the freedom to disagree with them. This is why, as far as possible, facts have been clearly distinguished from comments.

Philosophy and Democracy

> *Our path to the truth is through others. Either we attain it with them, or what we attain is not the truth.*
>
> Maurice Merleau-Ponty.

I

A RECENT QUESTION

What are the relations between philosophy and democracy in the world today? The question is an embarrassing one, but why? Simply because it is so broad? There's more to it than that.

The awkwardness has another source: each of these terms "philosophy" and "democracy" signifies too much. Both are overburdened with meanings, like two stacks of senses that have been piled on down through the ages. A juxtaposition of theoretical definitions, social representations, cultural and political realities, attractions and repulsions that make it difficult to use these words without qualification.

In our everyday usage, we think we can speak of a relatively homogenous thing: "philosophy". But what if this were an illusion? What if the ideas and intellectual approaches designated by the word had become totally disparate, totally impossible to unify? From author to author, from school to school, from country to country, and, even more, from one region of the world to another, it is easy to get the impression that the different meanings of the word "philosophy" do not match, may in fact be incompatible.

The same is true of "democracy". We know, for example, more or less what this term designated for Pericles in fifth century Athens; for Rousseau in the Age of Enlightenment; for Tocqueville in nineteenth century

American society; for Gandhi in the India of the 1930s. But what common kernel of meaning do these uses share? Between ancient democracy and modern democracy, liberal democracy and social democracy, are we not confronted by realities so different that use of the same term is more misleading than enlightning?

Are we dealing, then, with two words that "have more value than meaning, that have plied every trade", that are "very good for controversy, dialectic, eloquence" but not for systematic reflection and inquiry, to use the words written by Paul Valery concerning "Freedom" in *Regards sur le Monde Actuel* (1945)?

Well, no. There is no reason to share this scepticism. There are many reasons in fact to believe that there is an underlying unity relating philosophical investigations of whatever kind. Despite their extreme diversity, which is, in a sense, irreducible, it is neither by chance nor by error that they are called by the same name. Between the quest for wisdom and propositional calculus there is certainly a distance, but there is no break.

No more than there is a radical discontinuity between geometry and ethics, as Socrates pointed out in Plato's dialogue entitled *Gorgias*. In the multiplicity of different periods and cultures, we find, here and there, the same desire to apply reason to the problems posed by our condition, the same attempt to solve them through the efforts of the mind alone.

There are likewise good reasons to believe that the notion of democracy has an overall coherence. There is a central core to all the apparently incompatible configurations that are called "democracy": the idea of a society in which sharing (of power, tasks, goods…) is organized by ourselves, with no submission to laws other than those we have given ourselves.

But now we are threatened by a new embarrassment. Our minimalist definitions, debatable as they may be, have enabled us to save the question we began with: its terms do indeed have a referent. But there is still a problem: what are *the relations between* philosophy *and* democracy? This is more than a simple factual question. Merely noting the presence or absence of a coherent policy for the teaching of something called "philosophy" in one or another state claiming to be a "democracy" is not enough to give meaning to this question. This joint use of the two terms must itself be coherent to give an orientation to any further inquiry.

But their relationship is not immediately obvious. Although "philosophy" and "democracy" are originally Greek terms, it is clear that they did not necessarily go together for the thinkers of Antiquity. Need we recall that it was Athenian democracy that adopted the decision to put Socrates to death? Need we insist that Plato is harsh on democracy, whose principle he did not approve? Need we say that Aristotle did not consider it to be the best form of political organization?

Intellectual and political history do not advance to the same rhythms. The medieval monarchies of divine right did not prevent the development, in Christian Europe, of important philosophical schools. The imperial dynasties of China or Japan, or the warrior princedoms of classical India, did not shackle the flight of great speculative schools. And finally, celebrated democracies, such as that of the United States, do not grant philosophy an important place in their educational system or cultural life.

A catalogue of examples would be a waste of time. It is all quite obvious. Some of the great philosophers of yesterday and today were not democrats. Other regimes than democracy have allowed the development of philosophical work. Democratic countries do not pay more attention to philosophy than others. In short, at first glance, there does not seem to be any specific relation between philosophy and democracy, one that forces itself upon us as evident.

A close relation

But this is a mistake in perspective. When we take a closer look, we see that philosophy and democracy indeed have a sort of kinship. Not that they share a common identity. Nor are they in a relation of mutual dependence. There are four points, however, which suffice to show that they are closely related. These concern the very possibility of their existence, not contingent aspects of their concrete forms.

Philosophy and democracy both have a fundamental relation with:

1 – *Language,* for thought does not really exist until it is uttered, exposed, submitted to discussion, to criticism, to the arguments of others – this is true both for philosophical thought and for political positions in a democracy.

2 – *Equality,* for we do not ask others "by what right" they participate in a debate, we do not demand any authority or authorization, they need only speak and argue – this is true for political democracy (where all the citizens of a single nation participate in debates) and also, though in a different way, for philosophy (where all of humanity is concerned).

3 – *Doubt,* for if the quest for truth and joint discussion of the just is to be undertaken, immediate certainties must be able to vacillate, and we cannot live in a world of answers and credos, but of question and inquiry.

4 – *Self-institution,* for neither the philosophical approach nor the democratic community can be created by external decision, legitimated by authority "from outside", or guaranteed "from above"; both receive their strength only from themselves and are subject to no other authority than that of which they are themselves the source.

These features delimit a "common terrain", a foundation for both philosophy *and* democracy. Without being merged or absorbed, they have underground ties that are stronger than would at first seem to be the case. The quest for truth and the power of the people, while distinct, have correspondances. The loss of comfortable certainties is common to both. Claude Lefort notes this in his *Essais sur le politique*: " In my view, the essential point is that democracy institutes and maintains itself through a dissolution of the signs of certitude. It inaugurates a phase of history in which men are subjected to an ultimate uncertainty about the foundations of Power, Law and Knowledge, and the foundation of the relationship of one man to another, in all registers of social life."

But we have still to get a glimpse of the route that leads from this general kinship to the organization of an international survey. Let us try a shortcut. In the contemporary history of democracy, the French Revolution is an inaugural moment. It is not surprising that we find in conjunction here the exercise of free speech, the proclamation of equality, a rejection of religious authority, and the elaboration of a Constitution by the people's chosen representatives. It has no doubt not been sufficiently noted that this historic instant, part of the universal history of humanity, was also the moment at which the still unheard-of project was put forth of teaching philosophy to all. Helvetius wrote in *De l'Esprit* in 1758: "In all countries, the art of educating men is so closely linked to the form of government that it is perhaps impossible to make any considerable changes in public education without making changes to the constitution of the State itself". Perhaps the break that gave birth to modern democracy was necessary before the proposal to teach philosophy to all could be clearly formulated.

Paris February 25, 1795

Joseph Lakanal read to the Convention his *Report on the training of elementary teachers*. This was the day the French Revolution gave birth to the idea of philosophical education organized by the State with the aim of educating citizens morally and intellectually. Before this, the act of philosophical reflection was considered to be a private matter. A philosopher was supposed to have the right to express himself in public, but in his own name, and addressing himself to those who chose to share his inquiry. Thus, at the end of the seventeenth century, Spinoza claimed the right for each individual in a free country to "*teach publicly, at his own expense and at the risk of his reputation*". There was no conception of the State as organizer of philosophical education. Nor was there any specific role for philosophy in the education of citizens.

The appearance of these two demands – public education, and "education for freedom" – is linked to the emergence of a political regime founded on the existence of individuals who are free, aware, and sovereign. The constitution of a lay republic, the declaration of human rights, and the organization of public education are indissociable. In this spirit, the French Revolution aimed to put an end to inequalities of development that affected a citizen's capacities for judgement. Joseph Lakanal emphasized this forcefully. The text is worth citing, for it sketches an educational utopia whose goals are still relevant.

"For the first time on earth, nature, truth, reason and philosophy are thus to have an academy. For the first time, the most eminent men, in all areas of learning and talent, the men who until now have been teachers only of nations and of the centuries, the men of genius, will be the main schoolmasters of a people.... This source of light, so pure, so abundant, since it will emanate from the foremost men of the Republic in all domains, pouring from one reservoir to another, will spread from place to place over all of France, losing none of its purity in its course. In the Pyrenees, in the Alps, the art of teaching will be as it is in Paris, and will be the art of nature and of genius. Children born in thatched cottages will have instructors more skilled than those that could have been assembled at great expense for children born to opulence. We will no longer see in the intelligence of a very great nation small plots cultivated with extreme care amidst vast deserts left untilled. Human reason, cultivated with equally enlightened industry will produce the same results everywhere, and these results will be the re-creation of understanding in a people who will become the example and model of the world. [...] The resolution you are about to pass will mark a new era in world history."

What, in these words pronounced two centuries ago, can we still respond to today? Certainly not to the idea of a model people or an exemplary nation, nor to the idea that France is to play a unique role. The main problem is still that of inequality. Both within a single country and between the different regions of the world, the possibilities of exercising one's reasoning abilities and of learning to judge freely are not equally shared.

All human beings have an equal capacity to distinguish
the true from the false. Descartes reminded us of this,
long after Socrates' dialogue with the slave boy. But all
do not have the same opportunity to *exercise* this capacity. We are still faced with this necessity: to give to each
individual, everywhere, and as much as possible throughout life, the chance to make full use of his or her own
freedom. Likewise, the imperative of ensuring that
thought is subject to no religious or ideological censorship has an urgency that has not diminished with time.

Thus the basic goals are no less relevant. But time,
nevertheless, has taught us to be careful. We know today
that even universality is sometimes to be viewed with
suspicion. Is desiring to cultivate reason the same way
everywhere, expecting it to produce "the same results
everywhere", not in fact an attempt to reduce the differences that define the nature of mankind? How are we to
distinguish universality from uniformization? How can
we be sure that, under the aegis of reason and philosophy,
we are not setting up a form of imperialism? In speaking
of liberation and emancipation, are we not in fact instal-
ling a new form of guidance, or even subjection, all the
more efficient in that it is subtler?

We can take this still further. Are the Greek words *philosophy* and *democracy* not also Greek (or at least western) "things"? Do they have equivalents in other
cultures? Do they have truly universal relevance? Can
different peoples, differently organized on the intellectual
as well as on the political level, share common models
and still preserve the differences on which their own identity is based?

Questions thus arise which can be the starting point for
a world survey. For example: is the idea of philosophical
education universally relevant? How can it be defined, so
as to contribute everywhere to the training of citizens?
What would its goals and means actually be? In what
form can it be relevant to today's world? In what ways
can it be aimed at the greatest number of people? How
can it combine the use of traditional resources (books,
dialogues, courses) and new media (video, CD-ROM,
Internet)? If there does not exist, cannot exist, a "world

philosophy", can we envisage a "world use" of philosophies? If so, of what sort?

Today we must try to address these questions from a truly planetary perspective. At least, we must make a start, and see what happens when we try. We are not yet used to thinking this way, but it is the only way the crucial problems can be addressed, or simply recognized: philosophy and democracy *in the world*.

The birth of the world

Why is this approach necessary? It is because only now is the world truly coming into existence. No doubt people have always named, in most languages, by the term "world" or its equivalents, the organized totality of what is real. But until the twentieth century this totality was a postulate of thought rather than an everyday experience, since linking its far-flung parts to one another took considerable time. In reality, the links were extremely tenuous: it takes more than just ten travellers, or a hundred, or a thousand, to create real interdependance between continents and civilizations. As long as events did not have repercussions from one continent to another, what we today call "the world" did not really exist.

If we had to sum up in a few words the main tendency of the twentieth century, perhaps the following formula would be the least unsatisfactory: we are experiencing the birth of the world. Interdependance has increased unceasingly between the regions of the globe. During this century, and particularly in the last fifty years, the transformations of technical capabilities, international relations, and ways of life have not just disturbed reality, in spectacular fashion, they have created "the world" as an organized, intercommunicating whole.

Its parts are in a constant and direct relation of interdependence. Each event can have immediate and unforeseen consequences very far from where it occurred. Problems or solutions no longer exist only at the regional level, in isolation. "World" is no longer a synonym of "international", as the economist François Rachline has emphasized in his study for the programme "Philosophy and democracy in the world". A wholly new dimension, an autonomous process, an interdependence that is constructed rather than endured, make the difference.

The main causes of this birth are familiar to all: the economy and communication. Economic production and commercial exchanges have seen a development that is unprecedented in the history of mankind, and this interdependence has strongly increased over the last few decades. Moreover, in parallel, communication systems have been extended to cover the entire globe. In many areas – political, economic, social, military, scientific – anything important that happens anywhere on the planet is immediately communicated everywhere. Information technology has produced an "immediate history of awareness".

This is the perspective in which the survey was conceived whose main results will be summarized in the following pages.

The question of the relations between philosophy and democracy in the world, as we have just briefly seen, is therefore a recent one. It was not an issue a hundred years ago. UNESCO, since its creation in 1945, has greatly contributed to bringing it to our attention. It is appropriate to recall why, and how.

II

UNESCO AND PHILOSOPHICAL EDUCATION

The initial impulse

Even before the first General Conference, held at the Sorbonne on November 20, 1946, the preparatory commission had written, on June 21, that UNESCO's programme in philosophy should aim at two goals: *"1 – to place adequate international instruments at the service of the advancement of philosophical studies; 2 – to place philosophy at the service of the international education of peoples."*

As can be seen by reading extracts of the original document, reproduced at the end of this chapter, the spread of an international philosophical culture was envisaged from the start. One of the tasks proposed for UNESCO was that of "imbue the public mind a certain number of philosophical and moral notions to be regarded as a minimum equipment, and which are calculated to reinforce a respect for human personality, a love of peace, a hatred of narrow nationalism and the rule of brute force, solidarity, and devotion to the ideal of culture." But in order to submit recommendations and propose initiatives to Member States, a sufficiently precise view of the real situations and their diversity was needed. Curiously, if there was a domain where world-wide information was cruelly lacking, it was philosophy. The first priority was thus to obtain it.

From the beginnings of its activity, UNESCO realized that a task of this kind was eminently part of its mission.

For example, in May-June 1950, the General Conference, during its fifth session, decided to carry out "an inquiry into the place occupied by philosophy teaching in the different educational systems, the way it is given and the influence it has on the training of citizens" (resolution n° 4-1212). It was not clear just what the term "philosophy" referred to in different countries. In many cases, it was not known what texts, what authors, what ideas had currency under this label. It was impossible to make relevant comparisons of the different forms of instruction, or of the place of philosophical education in politics and culture.

This project, defined by the General Conference in its sixth session, in June 1951, can be considered the ancestor of the present programme "Philosophy and democracy in the world". The relevant services of that period, under the responsibility of Jacques Havet, prepared an 82-point questionnaire. It dealt both with the place assigned to philosophy in education and with its role in the cultural life of each of the Member States involved. This first survey did not undertake to cover the whole world. It was aimed at 21 States, chosen "for the diversity of the problems that the teaching of philosophy posed for each of them".

Some States did not respond. With others, the answers returned did not give an exact idea of the situation of philosophy in the country concerned. Out of the 21 States first selected, 8 figure in the volume prepared under the direction of professor Georges Canguilhem, published in 1953 by UNESCO: Germany, Cuba, Egypt, the United States, France, India, Italy, the United Kingdom. This first initiative furnished much food for thought and many proposals for action.

An international committee, composed of nine experts, met in Paris, from November 26 to 30, 1951. Each had prepared a report on the situation of philosophy in his own country. Some of these texts are still of remarkable interest, such as that of Eugen Fink on Germany or Georges Canguilhem on France. The collective volume containing them stresses the function philosophy can fulfill in the development of critical thinking and education for tolerance. It also insists on the role UNESCO can play in the development of intercultural relations, judged insufficient at that time, in the teaching of philosophy around the world.

Even if it was not continuously apparent, this initial impulse never disappeared. Many resolutions attest to the attention given by UNESCO to philosophy in general and to its place in democratic education in particular. For example, in 1978 the General Conference, in its twentieth session, adopted a resolution (3/3-3/1) authorizing the Director-General to "promote the role of philosophical study and the teaching of philosophy in the life of different societies". A new series of investigations and reflections was launched. It resulted in the publication by UNESCO, between 1984 and 1993, of five collective volumes concerning philosophy teaching and research, in, respectively, Africa, Asia and the Pacific, the Arab states, Latin America, and Europe.

Thus UNESCO's interest is neither recent, nor fortuitous, in the areas of philosophy teaching, its role in the transmission of democratic values, its educational potential in the training of free and tolerant minds, and its place in intercultural relations. The 1994-1995 survey is part of this continued activity.

Why today?

At the moment when UNESCO is celebrating a half century of existence, we see, all over the world, the re-emergence of fanaticism and manifestations of intolerance and hatred. Curbs on freedom of expression, intimidation, assassinations, and the many forms of violation of human rights are once again features of the day's news.

Not all are friends of peace. Not all are partisans of democracy. It would be wishful thinking to imagine that on these points there is general agreement. In official declarations, no one opposes these ideals. Astonishing but true, they have no opponents! But the consensus exists only in words. When there are decisions to be made, actions to be undertaken, things get more complicated.

This has not prevented those fighting for freedom, peace, and equality from changing the world. In recent years, the positive results of these struggles have been

considerable, and they are known to all. In counterba-
lance to the growth of intolerance and fanaticisms, we can
point to the progressive fall of dictatorships and new
opportunities for democracy around the world. Both pictures are accurate.

With so much movement, so much diversity, it might
seem that philosophical education is a mere straw in the
wind. But it would be too easy to assume that it has no
effect. On the contrary, it may be that the state of the
world today again allows us to raise a question formulated at the birth of UNESCO and left pending since then:
is it sufficient to promote the extension of science and
culture to bring about progress in democracy, peace and
solidarity? Or, on the contrary, must we accompany this
cultural strategy with a specific form of education for
peace? The problem was raised by Léon Blum, the joint
chairman, at the opening discussion: *"The war which has
just ended, and which was, in the description of Marshall
Smuts in San Francisco, an essentially ideological war,
'the greatest religious war of all time', has shown us how
education, culture, 'in the narrow sense', and science
itself can be turned against the common interest of mankind. Popular education, institutions of high culture, and
scientific research, were no less developed in Germany
than in the rest of the world. Thus it is not sufficient to
develop and improve them. They must be clearly oriented
towards this 'ideology' of democracy and progress which
is the psychological precondition, the psychological key,
for international solidarity and peace."*

Can the teaching of philosophy fulfil such a mission?
Can it even contribute to it? Is such a role in line with its
history and nature? Or would this be a betrayal of its
vocation? Is there not a risk that it would lose its essence
if transformed into propaganda for an "ideology", albeit
one that defends the right? But can it be enough to merely
cultivate reason, in liberty, for the world to finally see
peace? Is it conceivable that, without losing its capacity
to doubt and criticize, philosophy can become an arm
against evil?

The question was asked at UNESCO at its very beginning, and it is still being asked today. It is not a question

that concerns only UNESCO, or only philosophy. But it is not an accident that it has come up again, fifty years later, in relation to philosophy, for UNESCO is itself a philosophical institution. The foundations, the raison d'être, the goals of this organization are philosophical in nature. Indeed, even if UNESCO was not explicitly and directly concerned with surveys, programmes, encounters, publications, and chairs relating to philosophy, it would remain, because of the very project that motivates and justifies it, philosophical by essence. This needs explanation.

Philosophical institution

In 1942, the Ministers of Education of the Allied Powers planned the creation of an institution which would contribute, by its intellectual and moral action, to the building of a world from which fanaticism, contempt for others, and neglect of the "democratic ideal" and of human dignity would be banished. Were they engaged in law, politics, or, at least indirectly, philosophy? In November, 1945, the authors of the UNESCO Constitution, assembled in London under Prime Minister Clement Atlee, chose to place at the head of the preamble these words written by Archibald MacLeish, poet, librarian at the Library of Congress in Washington, and United States delegate: " wars begin in the minds of men and it is in the minds of men that the defences of peace must be constructed". Were they, in their own way, doing philosophy? Was this a moment of history when the usual distinctions between thought and politics were blurred, even suspended? According to all who were present, few assemblies have ever manifested such creative enthusiasm, such a deep sense of the historical and human importance of their proceedings, such quasi-messianic fervour.

The UNESCO Constitution, which for fifty years has remained its basic reference and the justification for its existence, is a philosophical text. What this means is not that it is a text prepared by a philosopher, or aimed at philosophers. It is not even a decisive document which, of itself, "advances" philosophical thinking, whatever sense we give to the notion of advancement.

What is important, in this Constitution, are the theses defended. It states, for example, that "wars begin in the minds of men", that "ignorance of each other's ways and lives has been a common cause … of … suspicion", that "the wide diffusion of culture, and the education of humanity for justice and liberty and peace are indispensable to the dignity of man", and that there exists an "objective truth". Let us put aside questions that can be raised about the exact way these theses are formulated, the relevance of the terms, or the ordering of the ideas. These debates will be pursued elsewhere. Let us just note that the text on which the existence and justification of UNESCO is based involves a set of philosophical theses, i.e., assertions.

These assertions amount to decisions. To state that there exists a realm of the spirit irreducible to economic conditions and constraints, to maintain that peace among nations cannot be based simply on agreements among leaders, to suppose that there exists a set of values that are, or can be, universally shared, by all mankind… This is not a mere repetition of facts that are in themselves obvious. People can uphold, in fact have upheld, theses that are exactly opposed, proclaiming the primacy of economy over culture, of politics over solidarity, of the relative over the universal.

It is, then, by its very nature that this institution represents a philosophical choice. The first article of the Constitution states that UNESCO will *"give fresh impulse to popular education and to the spread of culture"*, and suggests *"educational methods best suited to prepare the children of the world for the responsibilities of freedom"*. Training in philosophical thinking is clearly one of these methods.

MEMORANDUM ON THE PHILOSOPHY PROGRAMME OF UNESCO (24TH JUNE, 1946)

The present document has been drafted as the basis of discussion by the Letters and Philosophy Committee (Sub-Section for Philosophy). Its statements are in the nature of pure suggestions, which will undergo revision when they have been discussed and added to by members of the Committee.

I – UNESCO and philosophy

In the field of philosophy our Organization is faced with a situation which calls for effective action. In the interests of war, contacts were broken between philosophers of the different countries; the universities lived in a vacuum and students of different nationalities were denied the opportunity of working together; the international circulation of philosophical publications almost ceased. And, what is more serious, philosophical concepts were distorted and put by the totalitarian countries to propagantist use, while the philosophers of those countries were either compelled to serve the State or were muzzled; philosophical errors were freely stamped upon minds with insufficient culture to question them, and in this way the tradition of the dignity of man became in many countries a dead letter. Even the democracies had to mobilise all their resources on behalf of victory, and the principles which should underlie human life in times of peace were often relegated to a secondary place, eclipsed by the principle of efficiency.

We are tempted in the international field to pursue a policy of laisser-faire. Philosophy, we shall be told, has need of absolute freedom; besides, since it employs inexpensive material implements, it can easily do without much financial support; lastly, philosophical work is above all the fruit of solitary study. It will be further argued that the achievements of philosophers are of little interest to the general public and that it would be Utopian to claim their use in moulding the public mind and to put them at the service of peace.

Yet the fascist governments, in their propaganda, did not ignore philosophy. They found it necessary to proscribe certain doctrines and to foster and disseminate others, not only in order to give their regime an intellectual lustre, but also inseminate their doctrine into the whole nation. We cannot believe that a philosophical inspiration which we regard as true is any less suited to convince the public or is incapable of providing the foundations of a spirit of moral solidarity among mankind. The terms of the UNESCO Constitution relate to concepts which belong to the province of philosophy, especially moral philosophy. The first duty of our sub-section is to clarify these concepts and to foster in the philosophical world a powerful movement on behalf of the principles upon which our whole work is founded, and of the values which mankind must establish.

Accordingly, UNESCO will not propose only to resume and intensify the work already done with limited resources by the International Institute of Intellectual Cooperation, that is to say, to encourage contacts between philosophers of the different nations; it will endeavour to disseminate, apply and even popularise an international philosophic culture.

For its essential purpose is to educate the minds of all men to the ideal of human solidarity; in the field of philosophy it will try to imbue the public mind with a certain number of philosophical and moral notions to be regarded as a minimum equipment, and which are calculated to reinforce respect for human personality, love of peace, hatred of a narrow nationalism and the rule of brute force, solidarity and devotion to the ideal of culture.

At the same time we must not fail to do all we can to advance philosophical studies proper. For international collaboration between specialists, even if it is at a level beyond the reach of the general public, can and should, like the solidarity research to which it contributes, be the living source of the ideas which we propose to disseminate in assimilable form. As in science or art, so too in philosophy, culture does not merely consist in popularisation; such culture would stagnate, lapse into slumber and quickly perish; philosophy cannot become a fixed credo or a petty educational technique. Popularisation, however, with which we shall be particularly concerned, is the product of continuously fluid thought, which is not cut off from the average human mind, even if its lofty clime and technical character raise it above the general level.

In the field of philosophy, UNESCO must therefore set itself two aims:

(1) to place adequate international instruments at the service of the advance of philosophical studies;

(2) to place philosophy at the service of the international education of the nations.

Nor is there any doubt that the marshalling of the different philosophical traditions, on the one hand, and, on the other, the confronting of pure philosophy with the concrete problems of the modern world, are bound to give a powerful impetus to philosophical studies themselves.

II – The domain of philosophy

We spoke of "education". Now, UNESCO has an Education Section, and the teaching of philosophy to students of the subject or even to the general public lies within that section's field. Similarly the concrete study of man in society belongs to the Social Sciences Section, that of the powerful instruments for the spread of ideas belongs to the Mass Media Section; the study of nature to the Science Section, and books and publications to the Libraries Section. At first sight, therefore, the field of philosophy would seem extremely limited, and it looks as though we ought to confine ourselves to the speculative field of pure metaphysics, theoretical and normative ethics and individual psychology. Those studies are no doubt important and represent one of the peaks of western culture, and we must not neglect them. But obviously action on our part in this sphere could not contribute decisively towards the maintenance of peace and the ennobling of man. UNESCO must interpret philosophy in a much wider sense than that.

There is in fact no real domain of philosophy. Philosophy is not on the same plane with the other subjects; its field ranges to the frontiers not only of human knowledge but even of all human activity. Thus its scope is as wide as UNESCO's own.

It is not enough to fight against illiteracy: we must also know the books which men must read. It is not enough to work together at scientific discoveries: everybody must understand that the value of science lies not so much in its applications (especially its applications to war) as in the emancipation of the human mind and in the creation of a vast spiritual commonwealth above all clans and empires. As for mass media, these can be used for any purpose at all. Unhappily, it was not the illiterate countries or backward, uneducated or non-industrialised peoples which fomented the conflict from which we are now emerging, and who rejected our cherished ideal of the dignity of man. UNESCO does not propose to perfect technical processes, but to use them for certain ends, for the realisation and promotion of certain values. The ends and the values assigned to each Section are the proper matter of philosophy. If our activity is to have a meaning and to be fully conscious of its meaning, philosophers must accept their responsibilities in the modern world and attack the concrete problems. They will not be taking the place of the specialists in each field, but their achievements will have to crown the achievements of UNESCO by giving intellectual unity to all our work, by elucidating its principles and doctrine, and by basing them upon a coherent conception of modern democratic man. It will have in short to justify UNESCO. We shall have to examine in detail the relations of the Philosophy Sub-Section with the other sections of the Secretariat. We may say at once that we must not be content to encourage the pooling of pure philosophic research throughout the world by helping and advising existing institutions, coordinating their work and ourselves making their omissions. We shall also endeavour to draw the attention of philosophers to a

number of human problems the theoritical solution of which is
presupposed by the advent of a unified world. The essential field
of philosophy, as UNESCO sees it, is applied morals (though
founded upon a theoretical conception of man and not only upon
a scientific study which would furnish us exclusively with facts
and not with an ideal); it is the psychology of man as a social
being, of man at grips with a science of his own creation and
with the conditions of life in the comtemporary world; it is the
philosophy of history, which must enable mankind to understand better the significance of the crises through which it has
passed since this century began. Approaching these problems in
a spirit which is both objective and sustained by a solid conceptual framework, philosophers will be able to revert to the ambitious tradition of philosophy since Platonism and to play their
part in organizing the human Republic.

III – UNESCO's plan of action

Action by UNESCO must be twofold: it must encourage
international studies in philosophy; and it must place philosophy
at the service of civilisation.

I – ENCOURAGEMENT OF INTERNATIONAL STUDIES IN PHILO- SOPHY

UNESCO will make no claim to replace international or
national Philosophical Associations born of private initiative:
philosophers, quite rightly, are too jealous of their freedom of
thought to accept official control, even international; we must
respect those private efforts. At the same time we have a part to
play, especially in the circumstances which the war has created.
We must:

(a) Organize an enquiry in the different countries to ascertain
what existing international or national philosophical associations deserve our help and cooperation; what associations have
lapsed since 1939 and not yet resumed their work; and which
are without the contacts or resources for renewing relations with
the rest of the world. We must find out their needs and their
importance.

(b) Stimulate the efforts of active associations.

(c) Coordinate them.

(d) Provide them with facilities and, where necessary, with
instruments of work.

(e) Initiate work in the form of suggestions or recommendations or even by activity of our own.

(f) Fill up any gaps we may discover in the existing state of
affairs.

In the same way, UNESCO will have to keep in touch with the
universities of the different countries; it will have to respect their
autonomy, but can make suggestions and recommendations to

them and, if necessary, bear part of the cost of carrying out educational schemes on an international scale.

UNESCO will have to keep in touch with publishers of philosophy with a view to sponsoring the publication of rare works, some of which promise no financial return. With a view also to ensuring, through existing international reviews, the dissemination of important work done by philosophers in different languages, either in the field of pure philosophy or of philosophy as an instrument for better understanding among men.

Relying upon existing organizations, UNESCO might set itself the following tasks:

1 – To bring about or encourage meetings between philosophers of the different countries

(a) International congress [...]

(b) Restricted congress [...]

(c) UNESCO, for its part, will have to carry on the work of the International Institute of Intellectual Cooperation, which used to organize at its headquarters small meetings between a few especially eminent philosophers and thinkers on subjects belonging to the field of concrete philosophy. These meetings should be very carefully organized by UNESCO; beyond doubt they would result in positive conclusions more interesting to the public (anyhow the cultivated public) than the work of over-large congresses. We shall be examining the importance of such gatherings in the next part of our report (philosophy's part in the education of the public mind). [...]

2 – To act as agent for indirect contacts between philosophers [...]

3 – Issue of encouragement of international philosophers

(a) International bibliography of philosophy [...]

(b) [...]

(c) Publication of manuscripts at present difficult to consult or of classical works out of stock.

Various libraries possess works of classical philosophy now out of stock and philosophical manuscripts (e.g. the Husserl manuscripts now at Louvain), which are of great interest and which publishers hesitate to issue for financial reasons. UNESCO might either subsidize publishers of philosophical works for purposes of such publication or undertake to publish them itself, after consulting philosophers and philosophical societies in each country.

(d) Translations

UNESCO must put in hand a vast programme of translations, the preparation and publication of which it will subsidize or completely finance. Every year each Member State will forward to the Secretariat:

– a list of notable philosophical works published in its country and which it thinks worthy of circulation in other languages;
– a list of foreign classical or modern philosophical works which it would like translated into its own language.

Philosophers privately consulted by the Secretariat unanimously recommend that works written in a language of countries not belonging to UNESCO, even ex-enemy countries, should not automatically be excluded. [...]

(e) Reviews [...]

(f) Transnationum Index [...]

(g) International lexical of equivalence [...]

4 – Encouragement of international exchanges of teachers and students. [...]

UNESCO might institute scholarships for students of countries who particularly need to widen their philosophic horizon by direct contacts.

Visits by teachers of a few days or weeks.

Establishment of "Homes" of Philosophy: A teacher at the Sorbonne has recommended to the Secretariat that it should encourage, first in the big world capitals, and later in large university cities, the establishment of Homes of Philosophy, where visiting teachers and students would find board and lodging at reasonable prices as well as rooms for study, gatherings, etc. [...]

5 – Partial internationalization of universities and their specialization in the study of a particular branch of philosophy [...]

II – HOW PHILOSOPHY COULD PLAY A PART IN EDUCATING THE PUBLIC MIND

This would be a difficult undertaking. Philosophers, we know, are reluctant to have their thought subordinated to political vicissitudes. We would not ask them to interfere in political matters, but to pronounce upon questions of ethics and social philosophy.

1 – Definition ot the rights of man and, particularly, of the individual in the modern world

The Sub-Section of Philosophy would initiate the convening next year of a conference of philosophers, psychologists and savants, representing all races and the different cultures and continents, for the purpose of studying the principles to be established and the methods of educating Man in order that he may exercise the rights and perform the duties of free men under the new democracy. This suggestion has been submitted to the Secretariat by the Mexican delegation.

The United Nations have a Committee on the Rights of Man, with which we should have to collaborate in the calling of this congress. The latter will not be duplicating the work of the

Commission, since it will be concerned more with applications than with principles.

It would be essential that the Congress should consist of a comparatively small number of delegates, and of men and women firmly resolved to reach a final agreement – this to avoid the risk of intellectual wrangling.

At the end of this congress a rapporteur might be appointed to draft a philosophical charter of the rights of modern man, a charter which could be published in all languages and circulated widely in all countries.

2 – Study of the present state of civilization and the aspects of what may be called the uncertainties of the modern conscience, and of remedies therefore.

This task of re-education by an analysis of the collective mind is undertaken much more usefully through round-table discussion between a limited number of psychologists, sociologists, psychiatrists, and psycho-analysts than by big congresses. The best solution would be to suggest subjects for discussion and investigation at gatherings held under the aegis of UNESCO (see First Section, N 1). At the end of each meeting, the members would fix the topic for the next meeting; a rapporteur would formulate the conclusions reached; a small brochure would be published in several languages and circulated.

The following would appear suitable themes for discussion: nationalism, war, the sociological causes of neuroses, man and the State, modern sexuality, political liberty, love of humanity, the philosophic interpretation of history, materialism, technics and machinery in civilization, etc.

There is one subject for study which could be proposed in collaboration with the Mass Media Section, namely, the influence of modern media of information on the human mind. In the visual field the growth of an illustrated press, which puts images before words, is starting a human revolution comparable in importance with the invention of the alphabet or, at least, of printing. Further, the technique of the headlines and the fact that most people only glance at their newspaper lead to a certain mental inertia, allergic to free study, contemplation and freedom of conscience. There would be much to say about the importance of publicity technique in the training of the mind of modern man and about the dangers of this state of affairs to democracy. Finally, the spread of information by the radio and talking film, with their visual impressions, is a human fact of which the significance must be grasped and the ill effects counteracted.

The cinema, which by reason of its universality and power of suggestion is a privileged medium of expression, must be subjected to serious psychological and philosophical study, the results of which would be discussed at a meeting called by UNESCO. Useful guidance could be given to film professionals.

3 – Dissemination of publications on special subjects with a view to the formation of public opinion – not by crude and immediate propaganda, but by long-term education.

We have already spoken of booklets issued at the close of congresses or conferences.

It would be useful to as philosophers (selected from those interested in questions of practical ethics) to compose an ethical handbook for the use of secondary school pupils throughout the world or at least for their teachers. The use of the book would be compulsory, but it could be the subject of recommendations to governments.

It is through appeal of the young, who are often attracted by seductive, yet dangerous doctrine, that we can help to create an atmosphere of concord in the world of tomorrow.

4 – Recommendations regarding the training of elementary teachers

The citizens of the democracies are trained in the elementary schools; but not even the simplest philosophical concepts can be taught to young children directly. At the same time it is important that their teachers should have sufficient philosophical culture both to impart to their teaching (ethical and civic) a liberal and international spirit, and to be proof against the lure of dogmas founded upon the cult of violence or contempt for human personality. UNESCO might recommend Member States to give philosophical instruction to future elementary teachers and to base it upon books approved by UNESCO or on UNESCO publications, particularly the ethical handbook mentioned.

It has been suggested to the Secretariat that in these last two fields it would be well to proceed by stages:

An international journal would be started in several languages, in which teachers and thinkers in the various countries would study the relations between philosophy and education for peace.

Once launched, this Review would propose a programme of ethical teaching for primary and secondary schools bearing upon certain questions like freedom of thought, the spirit of peace, etc.

The next move would be to get this programme, which would consist of only a few lessons, included in the national curricula.

"Wars begin in the minds of men and it is in the minds of men that the defences of peace must be constructed." Our Philosophy programme, if we can put it into effect, will not yield an immediate return comparable with the effects of propaganda, but we may hope that, by working upon the youthful mind, it may gradually come to exert a deep and lasting influence upon mankind in its progress towards moral unity.

III

"Philosophy and democracy in the world" is a four-stage programme: 1/a survey addressed to all Member States of UNESCO; 2/ meetings of experts to develop proposals for action; 3/ preparation of specific reports on regions and themes; 4/ publication and exploitation of the data collected.

1 – The survey

This is aimed at collecting as much data as possible. A detailed questionnaire was prepared. The 82 questions from 1952 were reformulated, updated, made more precise, subdivided. After being tested by several experts whose remarks and suggestions led to the rectification of some details, the questionnaire, prepared in French, was translated into UNESCO's five other working languages (English, Arabic, Chinese, Spanish, Russian). Accompanied by a letter from the Director-General, it was sent for the first time in September, 1994 to 184 Member States of UNESCO, as well as to the United States, Great Britain and Singapore. It was sent a second time in May, 1995 to those States from whom no answer had as yet been received.

In July, 1995, substantial replies from institutions or individuals, had been recorded and analyzed for 66 countries in all, whose names are listed in an appendix. This is a relatively small number, if we consider that only a third (66 out of 184) of UNESCO's Member States replied to the questionnaire, but no doubt we should correct this ratio in light of the many "small states" for which the questionnaire, on the whole, had little point. Nor should it be overlooked that a fair number of countries were not able to reply, because of war, famine, or economic or political troubles. We can estimate that these two additional categories represent approximately sixty countries. Thus, of those in a position to do so, about one Member State out of two (sixty out of 120) replied to the survey.

For most countries, multiple replies were furnished. It should also be noted that there were responses from all regions of the globe. It is thus reasonable to suppose that the general tendencies that emerge clearly from this survey are valid for the world as a whole. As far as we know, this is the first time so large a set of data on the place of philosophy has been directly collected from the best informed sources. Thanks to the efforts of all those who collaborated to produce this documentation, we have begun to have a better understanding of the diverse forms in which philosophy is either actually present, or is desired to be present, in today's culture.

2 – Study days and proposed actions

The "second phase" of the programme consisted of two international days of study, organized by UNESCO at its headquarters (Place de Fontenoy, Paris) on February 15 and 16, 1995. They focused on the role of philosophy teaching in the education of the citizen. The main goal was a confrontation of the analyses concerning this question coming from different regions of the world. Another aim was to put together concrete proposals for international action. These days brought together 24 experts (professors, researchers, rectors) from 18 different countries. Their names and the conclusions of their deliberations can be found in the last section of this book. Their contributions are published elsewhere.

The participants in these meetings put forward 14 practical proposals for international action. They also addressed to UNESCO seven requests for forthcoming activities of the Organization in the area of philosophy. Among the initiatives stemming from this gathering, the most noteworthy is the declaration of principle adopted by the 24 participants. This "Paris declaration for philosophy" can be diffused and signed by all those who agree with its contents.

3 – Specific reports

The third source of reflection for the programme "Philosophy and democracy in the world" consists of working documents specially commissioned by UNESCO. Ten reports were prepared. They were intended to shed light on specific aspects of the situation of philosophy in one or another region of the world, or to clarify certain aspects of the current state of relations between philosophy and democracy, relating to the development of the concept of citizenship, or the birth of multimedia. These reports offer analyses and reflections that supplement and clarify in specific ways the data generated by the survey and the study days and are listed at the end of this volume. The complete reports are published separately. Here, significant extracts are reproduced, with the authorization of their authors.

4 - Publications

On the occasion of UNESCO's fiftieth anniversary, the first publications resulting from this programme have been prepared. First, there is the present paperback volume, available in French and English, and soon to be issued in Spanish and other languages. In addition a collective volume, whose French version appears first, presents the elements of the study days and the working documents.

A last word

I would like to add a few informal remarks about the documents and the people involved, citing no names, just a few personal comments.

Replies to the questionnaire came back to us in various colours, some typed, some handwritten, and in a variety of styles: some are written on rough, dull, easily torn paper, others on thick, glossy white sheets.

Some of the answers are typed on ancient typewriters, whose letters are no longer perfectly aligned. Others are prepared on computers, using sophisticated word processing programmes, laser printers, and a choice of fonts.

There are sheets with a variety of headings, from countries, universities, institutions.

The texts are in English, French, Spanish, Arabic, Russian, Chinese, and here also there is diversity, with fax Russian alongside old-fashioned typewriter Russian, hand-written Arabic alongside computer printed Arabic, native English alongside broken English (or approximate French). UNESCO is also, and perhaps first of all, a world dwelling, a crossroads of nationalities, languages, cultures. People do not meet here in the anonymity of silence and individual journeys. There are genuine encounters, through speech or on paper.

Some replies came back very promptly, almost by return of mail, with great haste, and perhaps enthusiasm.

Others arrived later, as if the authors were reluctant to send them.

Some that were announced never came. Some perhaps were lost (which would be surprising, but not impossible). Others just didn't come. Maybe someday they will...

Great diversity in the political situations: freedom, oppression, indifference, terror. Terror lurking between the lines, coiled in the spaces between sentences. Some replies, even if predictably so, were enough to give the shivers. The language of fear, monosyllabic, icy, stereotyped, no human there. Or, rather, sometimes, one senses, on the basis of next to nothing, a detail, a comma, an odd phrase, that this zealous bureaucrat, obedient, whom it would be absurd to judge harshly, is also a human being.

Then there were the warm, the naive, the clever, the exhuberant, the ambitious, the generous, the punctilious, the boring, the grandiloquent, the sardonic....

How much time it must have taken! Amidst all sorts of other tasks, sometimes in difficult economic or political circumstances, in overheated or freezing offices. With no remuneration and no benefit. Except for a common love for philosophy.

I often thought, as I worked, of those who took the time to fill in page after page.

Sometimes I would even imagine them, look for their towns on the map, wonder how the weather was, think about their classrooms, how they travelled to and from work, their students, the piles of papers to correct, their course notes. Sometimes my questions were odd: did they smoke? drink?

Some images came for no reason: I saw some dressed in grey, others in white or black, without knowing why. I thought of the extraordinary diversity of these individuals and their situations.

Those were the things I did not know, what I could dream about, sometimes, as a sort of minute compensation for all the things I would indeed never know.

But there are also all the things, and there are many, that I did know.

I knew that some of them met, that they organized special work sessions. I knew that they sometimes came from afar, that they discussed for days, that they cooperated, organized workshops or seminars. I knew that they reread the preliminary version of the reply, made corrections, weighed every word. I knew that they shared out tasks, did research.

Their responses taught me a lot. I spent many weeks in their company. I finally got to know some of them well, to recognize them in the shapes of their letters or the grain of their paper.

With no other knowledge of them than that emerging from these written or printed pages, I was able to see how all our correspondants brought to these replies their experience and their attention. I feel a deep gratitude for this, all the more real in that it is not personal: I am not grateful for myself, but for everyone, for philosophy, if you will. Just a step taken in the honour of thought. If this is not too high-sounding for such a small step. I would like them all to know this though, to hear of it, to be told about it, if this book does not reach them directly.

This gratitude creates an obligation, and a fear. The obligation to be faithful to their words, not to deform them, betray them. To try and render both their irreducible diversity and their points of convergence, and, sometimes, their underlying unity. The fear, of course, is of failure to do this. How is it possible to echo all of them, in so little space? How to know whether, even with the best of intentions, one is not mistaken in what one says in the place of others? How can one not feel such fear, given all that is owed?

I have often wondered before, during, and after this survey about the best way to report on it, about the most relevant guidelines were, and which vantage point offered the most extensive and precise view of the landscape. I have often taken paths which, after a while, appeared either too steep, or too flat.

I still feel that I have not shown everything, because of limitations of space, of time, of competence.

I have consulted a number of specialists, and tried to take account of their opinions, and their advice has often been precious.

I alone am responsible for the imperfections of the result.

How might they be remedied? There is no way.

QUESTIONNAIRE

I – Overall view of philosophy teaching

1.

(a) At what time was philosophy teaching introduced into the current education system(s) and how was this done?

(b) What relation was there at that time between the teaching of philosophy and the intellectual and political movements favourable to democracy?

2.

(a) Is philosophy teaching more popular today or less?

(b) To what factors can this be attributed?

(c) Can any relationship be established between this situation and political developments?

3.

(a) Generally speaking, is philosophy teaching the subject of a considerable amount of comment (whether favourable or unfavourable), indicating that the public attaches importance to it?

(b) What are the public's hopes and fears, if any, regarding this branch of teaching?

4.

(a) To what extent does the organization of philosophy studies depend on central government?

(b) What role is played in relation to philosophy studies by the following authorities: political (State or government), educational (universities or public or private institutions) and religious (churches or denominational groupings)?

(c) Do any other authorities exert an influence on the administration of philosophy studies?

5. What degree of uniformity is conferred nationwide on philosophy teaching by its administrative structure?

6. What appear to be the advantages and disavantadges of the current system?

II. Position of philosophy teaching in the various types of education

A. In general education

7.

(a) Is philosophy a special subject at the secondary level?

(b) If so, what form does it take?

8. If philosophy teaching is provided for the first time at the secondary level, what is the average age of the pupils when it is introduced?

9. What appear to be the advantages and the disavantages of the organization of the philosophy teaching at the secondary level?

10.

(a) Does philosophy figure among the various subjects students can study as part of their general education during their higher studies?

(b) Approximately what percentage of students receive a philosophy education during their university studies without opting for specialized philosophy studies?

11. If philosophy teaching is provided for the first time at the higher level, what is the average age of the students when it is introduced?

12.

(a) What appear to be the advantages and the disavantages of the organization of philosophy teaching at the higher level?

(b) Is it considered in university circles that an introduction to philosophy teaching should be provided at the secondary level or that it should be provided only at the higher level?

(c) What are the main arguments put forward in favour of each position?

(d) Who supports each of these positons? Where are their various supporters located? Are these debates reflected in public opinion?

13.

(a) Is philosophy taught in higher education institutions other than universities?

(b) Tick the types of institution in the following list where philosophy teaching is provided:
- training schools for primary-school teachers
- training schools for secondary-school teachers
- colleges of administration or diplomacy
- vocational colleges
- technical colleges
- art colleges
- religious seminaries and monasteries (give details of time-tables and programmes, if possible)

14. If philosophy teaching is provided for the first time in these higher education institutions, what is the average age of the students when it is introduced?

15.

(a) What are the effects of the provision of philosophy teaching in these higher education institutions? (List more than one, if appropriate)

(b) Can differences be detected between the philosophy tea-ching provided in universities and that provided in the above-mentioned higher education institutions? (List more than one, if appropriate)

B – Higher studies for students specializing in philosophy

16.

(a) Are there several stages in the training of students who chose to specialize in philosophy? (If so, please describe them)

(b) What is the normal lenght of higher studies consisting of a specialization in philosophy?

17.

(a) What criteria are employed to select students applying for this type of course?

(b) What prior training is required?

18. At what point can students specialize in one branch of phi-losophy?

19.

(a) What is the exact or estimated number (state which) of philosophy students?

(b) What percentage of the total number of students do philo-sophy students represent?

(c) What percentage of students studying arts or social sciences do philosophy students represent?

(d) What is the proportion of women among philosophy stu-dents?

III. The programmes

20. Tick off in the following list the areas that are included in philosophy teaching (show as accurately as possible differences between levels of instruction and types of institution):

- religious dogmatics
- philosophy of religions
- general philosophy, ontology and metaphysics
- theory of knowledge
- logic (propositional calculus, predicate calculus, properties of formal systems)
- philosophy of science
- language analysis
- value theory, general ethics, applied ethics
- general sociology, empirical sociology
- political doctrines
- political philosophy, theory of the State
- philosophy of law
- philosophy of history
- general psychology, experimental psychology, psychopatho-logy

- philosophy of the mind and cognitive science
- pedagogy, educational science
- anthropology, ethnology
- aesthetics
- history of philosophy
- other (specify)

21.

(a) Is definition of the limits of philosophy teaching a subject of discussion?

(b) Is consideration being given to extending or reducing the area covered by philosophy teaching? If so, what are the principal arguments put forward by each side?

22. For each level of education, indicate the core programme and the optional or elective programme (attaching, if possible, the official text of the regulations in force).

23. What place does the study of philosophy "classics" occupy in the programme?

24.

(a) Give by way of example a list of at least ten philosophers who are considered classic.

(b) Can the classics used in philosophy teaching be considered representative of the world heritage?

(c) Are there any imbalances or gaps? If so, is anything being done to correct them?

25. Does the general public understand that a knowledge of philosophy classics forming part of the world heritage makes an important contribution to understanding between cultures?

26.

(a) What place is occupied in philosophy teaching programmes by political theory, moral reflection and questions connected with the life of society? (State as precisely as possible the differences between levels of instruction and types of institution).

(b) Is this place changing? In what way?

27.

(a) What place is occupied in philosophy teaching by discussion of:
- tolerance?
- human rights?
- the democratic tradition?
- the foundations of international political life?

(b) Is this place changing? In what way?

(c) Are these questions tackled in a general manner or are they explicitly linked to particular situations somewhere in the world?

28.

(a) Is philosophy teaching in its present form thought to be appropriate to the living conditions and problems of today's world?

(b) Are any changes planned?

IV. Teaching methods

29.

(a) State which of the following methods are the most frequently employed:
- lessons given by the teacher
- expositions given by the students
- open discussion sessions
  . between the students
  . between the teachers and students
  . during class time
  . outside class time
- reading of classic texts, with or without commentary
- the writing of essays
- introduction to meditation and the philosophical life
- other (specify)

(b) Is the balance between these different methods changing? In what way?

30. Tick off in the following list the principal objects of philosophy teaching:
- the transmission of knowledge on the history of doctrines and systems
- the inculcation of moral principles
- the moulding of a critical sense
- the provision of methods of analysis applicable to a variety of areas
- other (specify)

V. The tools of the trade

31.

(a) Are textbooks used?

(b) If so, is their role changing? In what way?

32.

(a) Are some textbooks prescribed by official directives?

(b) Are some textbooks especially favoured by the students?

(c) When were these textbooks written? When were they last updated?

(d) What schools of philosophy do they represent?

33.

(a) What place do the textbooks in use assign to the various cultures?

(b) Are translations of foreign textbooks used?

34.

(a) Is use made of selected and annotated collections of classic texts?

(b) Are some collections of texts prescribed by official directives?

(c) Are some collections of texts especially favoured by the students?

(d) When were these collections written? When were they last updated?

35. Is the reading of the complete text of classic works of philosophy recommended?

36.

(a) What works of national, regional or foreign philosophers are most strongly recommended to students, by level of instruction and type of institution?

(b) What works of national and foreign philosophers are most read by students, by level of instruction and type of institution?

37.

(a) Are these classic works easy to obtain?

(b) How many classic works of philosophy are available in paperback editions?

(c) Are they available in libraries?

38.

(a) Is there a sufficient number of translations of foreign works of philosophy?

(b) Who takes the decision to have a work translated?

(c) Is there a programme providing assistance for translation?

39. Is a knowlege of certain languages required of philosophy students? Is it recommended? (State which languages)

VI. Teacher training

40. What kind of training must philosophy teachers undergo? (Give details, where appropriate, of differences in the training provided, by level of instruction and type of institution)

41. If there are several levels of instruction, how do teachers advance from one to the next?

42.

(a) Do philosophy teachers teach only that subject in the various types of institution?

(b) If so, are they required to have studied another subject in addition to philosophy?

(c) If not, what subjects other than philosophy do they most frequently teach?

VII. Competitive and other examinations, diplomas or degrees, competitions

43.

(a) Are there competitive or other examinations, diplomas or degrees that require, *inter alia*, a training in philosophy?

(b) If so, is there a large number of them? Do they constitute the rule or the exception?

(c) What programmes of philosophy apply in the most important instances?

44.

(a) Are there any non-philosophy diplomas or degrees the examinations for which include one or more philosophy tests?

(b) If so, what forms do these tests take (an essay, a written or oral textual commentary, a discussion with an examiner or jury, etc.)?

45. What competitive or other examinations, diplomas or degrees exist in the area of philosophy? What are the programmes for them?

46.

(a) In what instances must a dissertation be submitted?

(b) Are there several types of dissertation or thesis corresponding to different levels?

(c) If so, how do they differ?

47. In connection with the various examinations and diplomas or degrees, what methods are used to assess the work and ability of the candidates in the area of philosophy?

VIII. Philosophy teaching within the framework of other subjects

48.

(a) In the course of secondary-level or technical studies, etc., is philosophy taught within the framework of and along with other subjects?

(b) If so, specify the subjects concerned and the point at which this "indirect" philosophy teaching is given

49. Does philosophy play a part in the study of other specialized higher-education subjects? (e.g. philosophy of law)

IX. Philosophy teaching in political and cultural life?

50.

(a) What role does philosophy play in the moulding of citizens?

(b) Is philosophy education confined to a small number of people?

(c) Is philosophy education provided on exactly the same basis to both men and women?

(d) Does philosophy exert an influence on national cultural life?

51.

(a) Is the public interested in the role of philosophy education?

(b) Have any prominent figures recently expressed any views on this subject?

52. Outside the teaching profession, where are philosophy graduates to be found?

53.

(a) From what viewpoint are the programmes at the various levels of instruction prepared?

(b) Is there an officially recommended philosophical doctrine?

(c) Is there a broad consensus on specific philosophical positions?

54. What philosophical traditions are mainly reflected by the programmes at the different levels of instruction?

55.

(a) What is the relation betwwen philosophy teaching and cultural traditions?

(b) What is the relation between philosophy teaching and religious traditions?

56. What is the relation between philosophy teaching and the current state of scientific knowledge?

57. What is the relation between philosophy teaching and political and social ideas?

58. What appear to be the main philosophical orientations of the teachers?

59. If universities or teaching institutions enjoy any degree of autonomy, are there any major differences in approach?

60.

(a) What are the students' main concerns in the area of philosophy?

(b) How are these concerns changing?

61.

(a) Can it be said that philosophy teaching exercises an influence on students' thinking?

(b) If so, how can this influence be defined?

(c) How is it changing?

62. Is there a clear link between current or recently dominant philosophical orientations and the ideas that are most widespread in cultural and political life?

63.

(a) Are the national philosophical tradition and foreign philosophical traditions taught in the same way?

(b) From this angle, what are the advantages and disadvantages of the present situation?

64.

(a) Are philosophical exchanges with foreign countries considered an important factor for international understanding and solidarity?

(b) Do scholarships, temporary chairs and other facilities exist for philosophy students and teachers?

65. Have attitudes towards foreign philosophical traditions changed significantly in recent times?

66. What have the most frequent criticisms of the organization and spirit of philosophy teaching in recent years been?

67. Have major reforms of philosophy teaching been considered, adopted or rejected?

68.

(a) Have steps been taken to introduce philosophy teaching for adults? (Specify)

(b) If so, what appear to have been the results of these steps?

69. What role do the various institutions of society play in this area?

70.

(a) How many philosophy societies are there?

(b) What are the circulation figures for the principal philosophy journals?

71.

(a) Is the general public interested in the popularization of philosophy?

(b) Are there paperbacks or cheap collections on philosophy?

72.

(a) Do general-interest cultural magazines provide any coverage of philosophy?

(b) Is the influence of philosophical ideas perceptible in literature, the cinema, the theatre, criticism, the arts, etc.?

73.

(a) Do the press, radio and television provide coverage of philosophy? (If so, specify the form of this coverage for each medium)

(b) Do journalists provide certain philosophers with a platform to make original contributions on important topical subjects?

74. Is the influence of philosophy perceptible in political controversies?

75. How does/do the principal religion(s) view the relation between religion and philosophy?

76. Do the religious authorities express official opinions on the various philosophical traditions?

77.

(a) Is any influence exerted by philosophical movements on religious life or vice versa?

(b) If so, in which direction, and in what particular area?

78.

(a) Is access to philosophy teaching democratically provided for the greatest possible number as part of a general education?

(b) If not, are there any plans to change the situation?

79.

(a) What general effects does philosophy teaching, as it is presently organized, appear to have on customs and traditions?

(b) – on the principles and ideals of the community?
     – on the general outlook of the community?
     – on public opinion?

80. May philosophy teaching be considered essential in today's world in view of the social and technical transformations and worldwide problems of the modern age?

81. May philosophy teaching be considered to play a leading role in providing people with the means to search lucidly and in a peaceful fashion for solutions to contemporary problems?

82. What specific measures could be suggested to improve philosophy teaching?

This text, available in UNESCO's six working languages, was sent for the first time in September 1994 to all Member States of UNESCO and to a certain number of institutions and individuals.

UNESCO's Division of Philosophy had received, as of August 6, 1995, replies to this questionnaire from the following countries:

Albania, Argentina, Australia, Belarus, Belgium, Benin, Brazil, Bulgaria, Cameroon, Canada, Cape Verde, Chad, Chile, China, Colombia, Côte d'Ivoire, Croatia, Cuba, Denmark, Spain, The Russian Federation, Finland, France, Greece, Guyana, Honduras, Hungary,

Indonesia, Iran (Islamic Republic of), Italy, Jordan, Koweit, Lebanon, Liberia, Luxemburg, Malawi, Mali, Malta, Morocco, Mauritania, Nicaragua, Nigeria, Norway, Uganda, Pakistan, The Netherlands, Portugal, Qatar, The Syrian Arab Republic, The Republic of Korea, The Dominican Republic, The Czech Republic, Romania, San Marino, Senegal, Slovakia, Slovenia, Switzerland, Thailand, Tunisia, Turkey, Uruguay, Venezuela, Yugoslavia, Zaire.

Replies have also been received from the United States of America and the United Kingdom, which are not members of UNESCO.

Details concerning these replies are to be found at the end of this volume.

Four facts and their comments

I

A CREATION OF THE CENTURY

> "*Philosophy, from a more general point of view, is still the true teacher of citizens in a Republic.*
>
> "*It is, in essence, free search, independent thought, freed, not of all rule, but of all servitude. This makes it the necessary school for the exercise of all forms of freedom, because freedom of thought is the source and condition of all others.*"
>
> Amédée Jacques, 1848.

Overview

Viewed from afar, philosophy often seems old and outdated. There are several reasons for this. The present period is dominated by the rule of technicians and engineers, and most people, wherever they live, share the feeling that their future, even more than their present situation, directly depends on the mastery of technology. In comparison with practical training, whose results are immediately visible and measurable, philosophy may seem a useless old dream. Too general, too theoretical, too unprofitable... definitely a thing of the past.

This conclusion, clearly too hasty, seems to be suppported by other observations, of which the main one is the antiquity of philosophy. How can an intellectual activity that has not radically changed in the twenty-five centuries of its existence still be necessary for the children of the industrial revolution and of television? The men who led this sort of reflective life lived a very long time ago. They knew nothing of the requirements of efficiency. Mass production, electronics, the rapidity of world-wide exchanges were unknown to them. The writings of philosophers may be of interest to historians, but they have nothing to say to us, preoccupied as we are by the concrete decisions we have to make. Studies, work, politics, religion, love, family, art, sports, etc., are our main preoccupations (this list is obviously neither complete nor hierarchical).

Or else, we are totally occupied with survival: finding food, avoiding bombs, fleeing epidemics, the everyday lot of millions of human beings. In this case, philosophy is not just remote or useless, it is an inacessible luxury.

Famine and extreme poverty, war and its perversions, all situations of intellectual and physical destitution seem to rule out philosophical activity. Obviously, minimal conditions must be met for us to have the time to think about the notion of justice or the foundations of equality. And even if we have been fed, clothed, and housed, we still have to know how to read and write. Without these basic conditions, no philosophical reflection is possible. This is obvious, or so we are told.

But this statement is not entirely convincing. Important philosophies have been created and developed during some particularly troubled periods. Metaphysical and moral problems have been raised in societies perturbed by major economic ills. Theoretical debates have flourished among peoples whose sanitary situation was far from satisfactory. It would be totally unrealistic to imagine that only a society at peace, well fed, and vaccinated, is in a position to attend to philosophy.

In fact this view conceals another. Those who say that there are infinitely more pressing matters than the teaching of philosophy for most peoples, are not just thinking of the need to live decently and in security. Their main prejudice is their belief that philosophy is reserved to an elite. This idea is linked to the preceding one in a simple and obvious way: in all periods and circumstances, even the most troubled ones, small privileged groups have been able to escape the worst forms of misery. Requiring an availability of mind and time which presupposes that one's vital needs have been met, historically philosophy has been practiced by very small groups.

In this sense, it is undeniable that philosophy has, in all cultures, been reserved to a small elite. This was not necessarily by deliberate choice. Philosophy is not necessarily "elitist". If it were, it would share, always and everywhere, the conviction that the most disinterested and elaborated forms of reflection must inevitably be accessible only to a small number of people. It does happen to be the case that philosophy was, until recently, taught to a very small number of students. This is due to the way societies and education were organized, down to the twentieth century, in the different regions of the world. One might conclude that this is another reason why philosophy is a vanishing discipline.

In sum, if we simply take the most widely held preconceptions, the situation of philosophy teaching seems quite uninteresting: it is a field without a future, an archaic way of thinking, poorly adapted to this technological century, a useless subject, with nothing to contribute to today's young people, a lofty speciality, restricted to a few small circles of initiates: such, it is often believed, is philosophy. But it would be a serious mistake to accept such images. They are false, and in complete contradiction with the facts.

Indeed, the first finding of the survey organized by UNESCO is that philosophy teaching is a recent creation. What does that mean? Throughout history, philosophical texts have been commented in study programmes, students have practiced logical reasoning, etc. It would be odd to claim that philosophy teaching is a recent invention, when so many universities and intellectual centers in the Arab world, India, China, the West and elsewhere have handed down great works and their commentaries over the centuries.

What is new then? The organization by the States of philosophy teaching independent of any school or religion, developed by professors, usually employees of the

State, in a nationally defined cursus, and aimed equally to all the secondary or higher level students concerned. This specific form of philosophy teaching has only existed in the world for about a hundred years. It is in no way a survival of ancient culture or an archaic relic. On the contrary, it is a significant invention of the modern era.

As we shall see, this type of teaching began in the twentieth century in most countries of the world. In fact, in many states of Africa, Asia, the Pacific, or Latin America, such teaching was established after the second World War, and coincides with their independence, immediately following the adoption of a democratic and republican constitution. It is part of the establishment of a modern education policy.

So we must change our image, and stop believing that philosophy teaching belongs to the past. In fact it has only just begun, and has not been swept away by the engineering sciences, the social sciences or biology. On the contrary, it accompanies and often completes them. Nor is philosophy old-fashioned and outdated: the questions it deals with are still asked every day, and reformulated in every age, with the data appropriate to each new context. Instead of consigning the old philosophers to cellar or attic, it is better to try and see what tools they can provide to help us better understand our present situation and, perhaps, deal with it more appropriately.

It is also time to stop viewing the teaching of philosophy as elitist and reserved, by choice or by its very essence, to a happy few. Throughout the century, and especially in the last thirty years, the world tendency has on the contrary been towards an increasing democratisation of philosophy teaching, provided to as many students as possible. Thus many countries have created an initiation to philosophy in secondary schools, sometimes covering the last two or three years. Some have even experimented with the teaching of philosophy in primary schools. One of the first things we learn from the responses to the UNESCO questionnaire is that philosophy teaching, in the sense described above, has just begun to exist. It belongs to the twentieth century, and is related to the democratisation process. As we will see more clearly in the following chapters, it has accompanied our age in its most essential political and moral turnings.

The Survey Data

We can start with Africa in our overview of the answers to the first question of the UNESCO survey, formulated as follows: "When and how was the teaching of philosophy introduced into the current education system(s)?" This is appropriate because the introduction of philosophy teaching is most recent in the African states, often dating from the sixties. No reply mentions a date before the beginning of the century, and most indicate dates within the last fifty years.

It is often difficult to determine a precise year. Other considerations become relevant when we try make the chronology precise. We can take, as an example, the case of Mali. One of the responses states: "While the discipline had already been taught [...], it was introduced into our educational system only with respect to the colonial heritage. It appears in 1948, with the first final year classes taught at the Lycée Terrasson de Fougères (today the Lycée Askia Mohamed in Bamako)." But this is still the prehistory of philosophy teaching in Mali. At that time the country did not yet exist, and in what was then French Sudan, philosophy teaching "was still paternalistic, with a negative perception of traditional African thinking".

After independence, the education system was reformed "with the basic objectives of mass education and a rehabilitation of third-world and nationalist themes. The discipline of philosophy was mainly of Marxist inspiration". That is when philosophy teaching really began in Mali. But it was still not true philosophical education, but more of an ideological and political indoctrination. "After the military coup in November 1968, philosophy teaching in particular was the object of various conflicts and debates. The new authorities worked hard to suppress its militant roots and Marxist ideology. This orientation continued even after the recent advent of democracy, in 1991. The present educational system teaches philosophy in a more classical and pluri-doctrinal manner."

The provisional conclusion: in this African country, an open and pluralistic teaching of philosophy slowly began to be established only a quarter of a century ago. On the scale of cultural and social history in general, philosophy education seems here a quite recent invention.

With specific differences corresponding to the individual history of each State, the same major stages are found in other French-speaking African countries. In Cameroon for example: "Philosophy teaching in Cameroon began in 1948 and was thus part of the general picture of the relationship between the French educational system that of the French-speaking part of Cameroon. At the secondary level, the French system served as a model until 1977. Since then efforts have been made to decolonize philosophy teaching. These need to be continued. In higher education, philosophy teaching was introduced at the University of Yaoundé in 1963."

The response from Zaire describes a situation whose main features are similar: "In 1962, a general educational reform introduced a programme for secondary education, including, in the next to last year, a course in philosophy. Five years later, in 1967, the first finalists took a State examination in philosophy... The first university department of philosophy was not established until 1968." There are other examples, with different nuances that have still to be analyzed. For example, the response from Benin states that philosophy teaching has existed in its present form "for about the last 80 years". The response from Senegal notes that this matter "was introduced in Senegal in the thirties with the creation of general secondary education by the colonial administration". The response from the Ivory Coast states that "the teaching of philosophy was progressively introduced during the sixties. At the university, which was not created as such until 1964, philosophy was not independent of sociology and anthropology. During the seventies, philosophy teaching became autonomous, and there has since existed a Department of Philosophy. Philosophy has been taught since the sixties in the final year of secondary school. At the beginning of the eighties, the teaching was experimentally extended to the next to last year of secondary school."

Thus, according to the data from the French-speaking countries, there are some noteworthy differences, but the conclusion suggested is still quite clear: philosophy teaching was introduced recently, is still marked by the influence of the French educational system, and has quite recently been trying to move away from it.

The case of English-speaking African countries is different, since the Anglo-Saxon model does not attribute the same role of philosophy as does the French system. Taught only in university departments and not in secondary schools, this teaching, considered as specialized, was established even more recently than the teaching of philosophy at the secondary level in French-speaking African countries. Thus philosophy was introduced to the universities of Nigeria starting in 1966 (1966: the Universities of Lagos and Nsukka; 1967: the University of Ife; etc.). The response from Nigeria emphasizes that "of 36 Nigerian universities, philosophy is proposed as a diploma course in 10 universities". One of the latest departments of philosophy to be created was at the University of Port Harcourt, where "philosophy was introduced for the first time as part of the basic study programme in 1978" according to the response sent by Pr S. Iniobong Udoidem. Other replies from other countries indicate similar dates. For example: 1966 for the University of Malawi and 1968 for the University of Liberia.

In sum, there is no doubt that philosophy teaching in these African countries has been relatively recently organized or reorganized. It is still very young, still experimenting with its newly-found autonomy. Far from being a relic, a leftover from a dying, outdated discipline, it is in fact a new educational option.

The establishment of State-organized philosophy teaching is also recent in those Arab countries where it exists. The historical and cultural context is obviously marked by the existence of an age-old scholarly philosophical tradition. Springing from its own sources, it also prolonged Greek thought, whose texts it transmitted to Europe. The historical background, then, is particularly rich and goes far back in time. However, State teaching of philosophy, in the public, normalized sense which concerns this survey, only dates back a few decades, and sometimes less.

According to the responses received, philosophy teaching "was incorporated in 1925 into the educational system" of the Syrian Arab Republic, and in Lebanon, in 1946. In Tunisia, the chronology given is the following: "Secondary teaching: 1948-1956 in French in Tunisian and French classes (at the time of the French protectorate); 1956-1975 in French in Tunisian lycées. Since 1975 in Arabic, in lycées and teacher training colleges. Higher education: 1963-1980, mostly in French. Since 1980, two thirds of philosophy teaching is in Arabic and one third in French". The reply from Morocco reports a similar chronology: "Since independence (1956) and until 1973, philosophy teaching continued as it was, perpetuating the French system established with the protectorate. Since 1973, two changes have affected philosophy teaching. It is now taught in Arabic instead of French, and a programme of Muslim thinking has been added to philosophy as such." In the Islamic Republic of Mauritania, the present programme was implemented in 1983.

In other Arab countries, philosophy teaching is still only partially established. According to the reply from Koweit, for example, philosophy teaching at the secondary level is dispensed using an anthology of texts on logic, ethics and general philosophy; it existed prior to the creation of the University of Koweit in 1966. However, although a department of philosophy is planned, it does not yet exist. In other countries, philosophy teaching no longer exists as a separate discipline. Thus in Jordan, "philosophy was taught in the sixties but was stopped in 1965, and from then on notions of philosophy have been taught in other disciplines".

In Asia, also, schools of thought and philosophy teaching have existed since Antiquity, of a scope and depth that the Western world, in general, still has not measured at its true value. Here again, however, the very ancient existence of diverse forms of philosophy teaching should not be confused with the very recent creation of state-organized instruction. In Pakistan, as in India, the present system of philosophy teaching was established in 1947, the year of independence and partition. During the twenties and thirties, the teaching of philosophy had begun to renew itself in Indian universities, under the impetus of great intellectual figures like Dasgupta and Radahkrishnan. In India, in conformity with the wishes of the 1951 Conference of philosophy professors, there are no programmes imposed by central authorities or national directives. However, a 1978 official report emphasized that philosophy teaching must be an integral part of education.

In other Asian countries, the teaching systems as they exist today were introduced soon after the war: 1947 for Thailand, for example, and 1946 for the Korean Republic, which in 1983 reestablished philosophy teaching at the secondary level. It had been abolished shortly after first being introduced. In Japan, the reform instituting philosophy studies in their present form was implemented just after the Second World War. The Confucian and Buddhist philosophical traditions had begun to come into contact with western sources in the Meiji era (after 1868, especially at the Imperial University of Tokyo), but the most important changes are only half a century old.

The response to the UNESCO survey from the Institute of Research in Philosophy at the Social Science Academy of the Chinese Popular Republic states: "Since the fifties, a number of universities have created a department of philosophy, and, more generally, have offered instruction in philosophy." It will no doubt be remarked that not the same things are taught in Peking and Seoul, for example. The terms "philosophy" and "democracy" themselves obviously do not refer to the same concepts in these two places. There will be discussions and attempts at analysis of this point further along. The only thing we would like to point out here is the "newness" of the teaching – whatever realities it covers – in quite different countries and educational systems.

For the Russian Federation, the situation is more complicated. The problem here is to decide what event of recent history is to be considered the founding moment of the present situation. According to Professor Reuben

Apressian of the Institute of Philosophy of the Academy of Sciences in Moscow, one has to go back to the mid-fifties. What, up to that time, had been a single teaching structure, named "Elements of Marxism-Leninism", was divided into several distinct disciplines by decision of the plenary assembly of the Central Committee of the USSR's Communist Party. Along with Political Economy, and the History of the CPSU renamed "the history of scientific communism", there appeared a unit of Philosophy, under that name: "Although the structure and the programme of philosophy teaching, practically identical for all students, for some time would still bear the marks of Stalinism, philosophy, in its newly-won autonomy, reflected the tendencies toward post-Stalinist liberation and a certain democratisation of political and social life in the USSR." However, it can also be argued that the present organization of teaching is much more recent; as the reply of Professor Dobrokhotov puts it: "The educational system in the Russian Federation today is the product of gradual and still ongoing reforms which began in 1985 with 'perestroika', and became more radical after the failure of the 1991 putsch. Through a series of decisions, the ministry of higher education (the Russian Federation State Committee for Higher Education) abolished the old system, in which every university establishment had to have 'ideological' chairs: the history of the CPSU, dialectical materialism, historical materialism, political economy, scientific communism. The institutions were given the right to choose freely the humanities portions of their programmes. This led to some legal confusion since previous legislation imposing compulsory subjects in philosophy have not yet been formally repealed. In practice, the Ministry requires the teaching of philosophy or what is currently called 'culturology' (the history and theory of world culture)".

In the former Republics of the USSR, now autonomous states, it seems the situation of philosophy teaching is still unclear. Unfortunately, it is not possible to give sufficient information on this, since none of these states responded to the UNESCO questionnaire, except the Republic of Belarus. It is quite understandable that these countries in

the midst of being reorganized, with innumerable problems to be solved, were not able to reply to a long and
demanding questionnaire. However, this gap, which will
no doubt soon be filled, is all the more regrettable today
when it is a matter of great interest what consequences the
political and ideological changes that have occurred in
these States will have on philosophy teaching.

No doubt the political upheavals make it impossible to
give a clear answer to this question at present. It is significant in this respect that the three replies to the questionnaire from the permanent delegation of the Republic of
Belarus to UNESCO leave unanswered the question
concerning when the current system was introduced. The
current period of change makes it practically impossible to
provide information on this point. It is as if philosophy
teaching has been left "hanging", neither eliminated nor
reorganized, left to the initiative of the teachers and depending very largely on their personal audience. According to
T. A. Gorolevitch, of the Institute of Philosophy and Law
of the Belarus Academy of Sciences, "a positive change
has occurred, the ban against the teaching of non-marxist
western philosophy has been lifted". In spite of everything, it seems difficult to measure the real scope of the
change: "From incomplete data", the same reply states, "it
would seem that it is mostly the same teachers who formerly specialized in Marxism-Leninism who are teaching
the "new" philosophy. And even now this tradition apparently occupies the first place in their teaching". This judgement is corroborated by that of S. I. Sanko, Director of
studies at the Institute of Philosophy and Law of the
Belarus Academy of Sciences: "On the one hand we note
a tendency to diversification of what is taught. On the
other hand philosophy as such is often taught now by
those formerly trained to ensure the smooth functioning of
the ideological mechanism. This fact cannot but place philosophy in an ambiguous position." Without prejudging
the detailed content of the information concerning other
former republics of the USSR, it is very probable that ana-
logous features will be found in specific contexts.

The major observation, in those countries which no longer support communism, is the quite recent possibility of

diversified and pluralistic philosophical reflection. This is just beginning to appear, after a long period of monolithic dogmatism. In the educational system of the USSR of the sixties and seventies, states Ruben Apressian, "the teaching of philosophy was considered an important aspect of the ideological training of the population". Marxism-Leninism alone was taught. Philosophy seems to have had no autonomy, not even a relative one, with respect to political indoctrination. "Until the eighties, philosophy as a university discipline was considered to be part not of the humanities but of political science."

This change can evidently be found in all European countries that used to belong to the Soviet block. The replies from these countries date the introduction of philosophy teaching in its present form from 1989 or 1990. In Hungary, for instance, "in 1989 dialectic materialism, historical materialism, and scientific socialism were eliminated from higher and secondary education, and instruction was set up in the universal history of philosophy, sociology, politology, and ethics." In Bulgaria, where they "have been studying philosophy for a hundred years, since the creation of the University of Sofia, St. Clement of Ohrid" it can also be stated that "the present state of teaching dates from 1990". The same is true of the Czech Republic: the texts of the programmes that now govern the teaching of philosophy date from November, 1989.

In Albania, according to the reply of professor Artan Fuga of the philosophy department of the University of Tirana, the period from December 1990 to 1992 "saw the flourishing of the most diverse political, philosophical, and artistic ideas.... In newspapers, public meetings, everywhere, it was observed that the cultural and philosophical isolation of the country had harmed Albanian culture, broken all ties with modernity and the development of the western world. Economic poverty was accompanied by obvious backwardness in the social sciences, and particularly in philosophy." It was thus necessary to create, almost from scratch, and in particularly difficult conditions of penury, a programme of instruction in philosophy. This, it seems, was not done without hesitations and conflicts. "If, in the streets, victory over Marxist-Leninist philosophy was being celebrated, notes Artan Fuga, in the halls of the university they were demanding the entire elimination of philosophy, because it had taken over all study of society and had unjustly replaced sociology. The criticism of philosophical Stalinism was more or less assimilated to a refusal of all philosophical thinking. In September 1992, the activity of the Faculty of Philosophy and Sociology was even suspended for a year by the Minister of National Education."

It should therefore not be imagined that the bases of philosophy teaching can be easily introduced overnight, in countries where an authoritarian regime has long been dominant. Instead the work on a new structure begins. A transitional period, perhaps with conflicts and backtracking, seems inevitable. A society as different, in history and culture, from the countries of central Europe as Brazilian society seems to have followed a similar route with respect to philosophical instruction: a relatively discrete institution, an authoritarian transformation, a recent renewal. As the reply to the UNESCO questionnaire, from the department of philosophy of the University Rio Grande do Sul, says, the teaching of philosophy in Brazil, which was introduced in the twentieth century, in the nineteen thirties, as the main universities of the country were being created, is now "governed by law 5692 of August 11, 1971, which defines the basic guidelines of primary and secondary level teaching. This legislation, whose origin goes back to the most repressive period of military dictatorship ... stresses the professional orientation of secondary education, introduced compulsory instruction in moral and civic education, and made philosophy an optional subject.

This attempt to replace free reflection by compulsory morality lasted only ten years. As the reply from the University of Brasilia notes, the teaching of philosophy "was reintroduced in 1982 with the new law on secondary education, which eliminated compulsory professional instruction and left the possibility of including 'philosophy' to the decision of the establishments and teaching structures of the different states".

In spite of the great diversity of replies and concrete cases, one constant emerges from the answers from Latin America: a system of philosophy teaching was set up in the nineteenth century colonial period, and has been reorganized over the last fifty years. The details of this reorganization obviously differ with political circumstances, but these two features - an "old" beginning and a "recent" reorganization - are to be found in the replies from Argentina, Chile, Colombia, Cuba, Honduras, Nicaragua, the Dominican Republic and Venezuela.

The situation in western Europe is obviously different: philosophy teaching organized by the State appeared there decades before it did in other regions of the world. It has served as a model for more recent creations, which often began by copying it, to the detriment of their cultural specificity, before seeking their own way. European philosophy teaching was long considered to be the only legitimate kind, but this predomination seems to be lessening. It should yield to the invention of new ways of philosophizing, which take into account both the diversity of the cultures involved and the great conceptual heritages. Europe's philosophical past is not the only significant one, but it is still considerable, and who would doubt this?

This European "philosophical heritage" is noteworthy for its age and continuity. From Athens to Oxford, from Miletus to Seville, from Rome to Paris, there has existed for more that twenty-five centuries, almost without a break, a tradition of philosophical education, renewed from one century to another by the great works that constitute its history. In spite of the diversity of languages and styles, it is true that, under the name of philosophy, Europeans have virtually never stopped teaching, commenting on texts, conducting debates and "disputes", and producing books of all sorts. For twenty-five centuries! The organization of philosophy teaching by the State represents, of course, a profound change. And this modification is also a recent one: for many European countries, it goes back to the nineteenth century and no further. But the changes that are nearer to us were made against the background of a very long history, and this is worth mentioning.

In spite of the great age of philosophical education in Europe, in general or only as state-organized teaching, the fact is that its current situation is the result of more or less recent changes. For those countries where the teaching of philosophy at the end of secondary-level studies goes back a century or more, we note that a new organization has been introduced more recently. Thus in France, where this institution goes back to the initiatives of Victor Cousin in 1844, a redefinition of the spirit and methods of the "philosophy class" was introduced in 1925 by ministerial instructions that are still valid. Among other things, these state: "It is in the philosophy class that students are given their apprenticeship in freedom by exercising reflection and it can even be said that this is the proper and essential goal of this teaching." In Italy, where the introduction of philosophy teaching during the last three years of secondary education goes back to 1859, the programmes and methods were reformed by Gentile in 1923, aimed at an approach to the study of philosophy focusing mainly on the history of doctrines.

In many European countries, the decision to create philosophy courses at the secondary level is rather recent. In Luxemburg, it goes back to 1968 and calls for compulsory instruction in the last three years. In Denmark, the new system was introduced in 1987, as an option available for either the last two or three years of school. In the Netherlands, after an experimental period which lasted seventeen years, philosophy was adopted in 1990 as an optional examination subject for pre-university education.

Nevertheless, a reorganization of such depth that it can be considered a "recent creation" derives its full significance for the teaching of philosophy in Europe in the countries which have seen profound political changes. This is the case of Portugal, since 1974, and Spain, since 1975, which embarked on the process of reconstruction of democratic public and intellectual life after long years of dictatorship. This renewal obviously had important and numerous repercussions on the teaching of philosophy, which has long existed in Portuguese secondary education (covering the last two or three years of instruction) and Spain (the last year).

It would be useful to compare the unique case of
Germany, where reunification caused changes that have
been insufficiently studied, to the replies from Albania,
Bulgaria, Hungary, The Czech Republic, Romania,
Slovakia and the other countries emerging from the communist era. These changes are analyzed in a study prepared especially for the UNESCO programme "Philosophy
and democracy in the world" by Johannes Schneider
(University of Leipzig).

To this first brief overview, should be added the exception represented by the United States, where philosophy
teaching does not occupy the place it has in other regions
of the world. It is neither a recent creation nor organized
by a central authority. As is indicated in the replies to the
UNESCO questionnaire, there is a philosophical presence, stronger than is often thought, in the history of
American culture and, above all, of political life. The
names of Benjamin Franklin and Thomas Jefferson suffice to show this. We might also add Emerson and Dewey.
There is also a non-negligeable presence of philosophy
teaching in university programmes. But that is about all,
and there is no way to draw a correspondance between the
situation in the United States and that just described for
the rest of the world.

That is, there is no trace in the American system of a
comparable transformation in the organization of philosophy teaching to that found in the nations of the rest of
the world. As professor Richard Rorty notes in his reply,
"philosophy is a quite unknown subject in the United
States. Most faculties are hardly aware of the existence of
a philosophy department in their university. There is practically no public discussion of what is happening in philosophy".

Perhaps this situation should be related to the fact that
democratic life, and, as it were, the "philosophy of democracy", have played, in American society, a different role
than they have in Europe and the other regions of the
world. Could it be that when a philosophy is put into
practice it is useless to teach it? This is merely a hypo-
thesis. To this should be added what is explained by the
development of American philosophy itself. With respect

to the point of interest here, we can distinguish two currents, one "technical" and the other "popular". The first, which became dominant in the twentieth century, considers philosophy to be a highly specialized activity. On this view, its teaching should be reserved to a small number of students and can have no relation to the general public. Just as mathematicians do not speak of their work on television or in newspapers, so philosophers have nothing at all to say outside of the small circle of specialists. Philosophy, dealing with problems of logic, and the validity of arguments, is a scientific discipline, which is developed in research institutions, specialized publications and learned conferences. Its efforts do not concern the man in the street, who can no more understand them than he can claim to participate in the research of physicists, chemists, or biologists.

This attitude has in fact shown a tendency towards greater flexibility even within the realm of analytical philosophy, which today more readily takes up questions of moral and political philosophy than it did even twenty years ago. The existence of a second current in American philosophy is becoming more clearly perceptible. This current considers that philosophy has a liberating role, and that the question of its place in general education is highly relevant. Emerson, in particular, in the last century, had insisted on these points, and it has recently been echoed in the work of the philosopher Stanley Cavell.

A first analysis

On closer inspection, the teaching of philosophy is still quite young, and might have a bright future. This youth corresponds to the recent birth, throughout the world, of state-organized philosophical instruction. In most countries, as we have seen, only twenty, thirty, or at most fifty years have passed since the first programmes were created and the first courses taught. In the countries where this tradition is older, it rarely goes beyond a hundred years. In the history of thought, and of mankind, this is a very short interval, so it is not misleading to speak of youth.

To see this, a global viewpoint is indispensable. In considering each country in isolation, one might judge that philosophy is more or less out of phase and unrelated to the reality of what is happening. This impression disappears when we can adopt a planetary view. The perspective changes, and we now see, almost everywhere, a recent, more open form of philosophy teaching placed, with very few exceptions, under the responsibility of the State.

This responsibility, wherever it exists, is unshared and quite extensive. In all the replies received – except those coming from the United States – it seems clearly to be the case that the State is responsible for almost everything in the organization of this teaching. More or less directly, it develops programmes, fixes schedules, trains teachers, recrutes and pays them, validates examinations and diplomas, etc. It can of course be observed, justifiably, that this is so for all areas of teaching and all fields of knowledge, so why draw any specific conclusions for philosophy?

Mathematics, for example, or the natural sciences, have been taught for centuries in diverse forms. Only recently, in most instances during the twentieth century, have they been included in a national educational system that is standardized and supervised by a secular and republican national authority. This observation can clearly be extended to all branches of learning. It certainly justifies detailed analysis of how the contemporary State has been taking control of education. But no one would consider questioning the profound changes in mathematics or the natural sciences, following or caused by this development. Nor would anybody think of asking how much mathematics can now contribute to the progress of democracy. What, then, is special about philosophical education?

If the answer could simply be "nothing", then the questions inspiring this survey would have no object. There would be almost nothing left but "technical" problems of administrative or financial organization, if the teaching of philosophy was to be limited to topics in the history of ideas, the rudiments of logic or some form or other of civic instruction. No doubt, it can include such things, which are clearly not useless. But it cannot be reduced to these. What philosophy teaching involves is much simpler, even though it is difficult to name with a single word. No doubt if we speak, as in the UNESCO Constitution, of "the minds of men" we are pointing to what is involved. But doesn't mathematics, or any other science, also concern "the minds of men"? No doubt they do, but not in the same way, or with the same meaning of this term. The other disciplines do not have the ambition of involving the mind in all its dimensions.

Philosophy, on the other hand, always has as its horizon the totality of what is. In the most common conception of philosophy, whatever the doctrine or culture, there is the desire to avoid separating the different aspects (individual or collective, universal or relative) of "the minds of men". In our first look at the replies to the UNESCO survey we have seen, independently of any general findings, the disparity of philosophy teaching around the world. There are obviously major differences between those states for which Marxism-Leninism remains the official doctrine, those which are busy getting rid of communist ideology, those which have recovered democracy after military dictatorships, those which have lived in the continuity of uninterrupted liberalism, etc. But in spite of these disparities, the founding project of any philosophical programme is that of understanding, as fully as possible, all manifestations of reality. It is in this sense that philosophy necessarily deals with the "mind". Here, this term englobes the processes called "spiritual", as well as those called "psychic", "ideological", "mental" or "cultural", even though these terms clearly do not refer to the same registers of reality or imply identical theoretical frameworks.

But this observation does not suffice to clarify what motivates philosophy, what it wants, what it demands and what keeps it alive. The desire to know what animates any philosophical activity is related to a demand for freedom. By definition, what this freedom will create cannot be predicted. In this sense, the very existence of philosophy, its persistence, its renewal, constitute, at heart, "something obscure", as Stéphane Douailler has observed in a study prepared for the programme "Philosophy and democracy in the world". This is not an obscure use of specialized vocabulary, or even of the complexity of the questions themselves. What is obscure is the very motive that would allows us to account for the existence of philosophy. This is no doubt where its most fundamental link with freedom resides. No one knows what a free being is capable of. And no one knows what thought is capable of, when it can develop and express itself without fear.

These brief remarks are enough to help us see the central paradox of state-organized philosophical instruction. The task of the State should be to set up as well as possible the conditions for an intellectual activity which aims to encompass the totality of what is thinkable and which, at the same time, must remain free, and in the first place free with respect to the State itself. The requirement is perfectly clear in principle, but we are all aware how difficult it is to apply in practice. Between the formal organization of teaching and the ideological orientation of its content, the frontier is often not clear. This is why philosophy must continually fight against its own institutionalization. This question clearly does not arise in the same way for mathematics nor for any other discipline.

Finally, philosophical reflection seems to be on the rise. It is in a period of reconstruction. This is the case in the states which are currently in a phase of reinvention of democratic life. Keeping in mind that we must avoid oversimplifications, we can sketch a typical evolution that may correspond to many real cases: first philosophy teaching is introduced more or less artificially and marginally, either by being set up by a colonial power, or else by taking as its model a foreign educational system. An authoritarian regime then takes power. It maintains the subject, but transforms it into a sort of official indoctrination. The freedom to criticize and the openness of mind which are the essence of the philosophical stance are forced to yield to state dogmatism. Propaganda and mental conditioning are substituted for reflection. Then, this authority, which imposes a dogma and does not hesitate to use censorship, intimidation, and even terror, collapses more or less suddenly, and is succeeded by democracy. In the ensuing pluralist ferment, the teaching of philosophy appears as it is: needing to be reconstructed.

It is marked both by the role of resistance it was able to play in clandestine opposition and by the heritage of the official doctrine it was responsible for disseminating. In one sense, it has still to be invented. Some are persuaded that the strengthening of democracy demands a renovation of philosophy teaching and studies. Others think that economic and social needs are so pressing that this can wait. In any case, philosophical education is, as it were, in convalescence from dogmatism. It is trying to find itself, asking itself about its function, questioning its relation to the society being born. It lacks means, information, books, and international exchanges. It is not simply a recent creation, basically complete, whose implantation and functioning are still imperfect, due to lack of time or money, but a creation coming into existence. The implementation of philosophy teaching should be considered as a process now being launched, or relaunched.

The above sketch of the passage from an authoritarian regime to democratic pluralism, and the parallel development of philosophy from dogmatism to free reflection, applies to numerous and disparate countries. The pattern can be found, with all sorts of nuances, in the republics of the former Soviet Union, now independent states, in the countries of ex-Socialist Europe, in many African countries where the marxist model was dominant, but also in many countries of Latin America and Asia which are newly building democratic public life after periods of military dictatorship.

Philosophy is coming back, after the strong-arm regimes and the terrors, at the same time as democracies are being reborn. But it would be a mistake to simply assimilate philosophy and democracy to one another. Their relation, as we shall see, is more subtle.

ECONOMY AND PHILOSOPHY

François Rachline

From the economic point of view, the twentieth century is that of interdependence[1], of individuals, companies, and nations. At the start of hostilities in 1914, this interdependence was just beginning to be felt. When the Berlin wall fell, on November 9, 1989, it was spectacularly visible. Between these two high points of a century full of noteworthy events, the world was not just totally changed, it became the world. Politically, economically, socially, it is no longer possible for something to happen at any point on the surface of our globe that the rest of the planet can really ignore. Information and telecommunications technology have reduced space as they have created an instant history in our minds. These changes have been accompanied by an unprecedented development of production and world-wide exchange.

This development has not been ignored by thinkers. They have also had to envisage the twentieth century from a global point of view, following the paths blazed by Kant, Hegel, and Nietzsche. In particular, philosophy cannot ignore the tendency towards universalization of the market economy, on the one hand, and the creation of international organizations which outreach and transcend national states. This article will deal with the correspondance between these two developments.

(This text studies the evolution that has lead from a "passive interdependence" to an "active interdependence" in the second half of the twentieth century, and the passage from the stage of international economic exchange to that of the global economy. It also focuses on the fact that this globalization has been accompanied by an attention paid by industrial production to singular situations. The last part of the article compares the creation of an European central bank with certain features of contemporary philosophical thought. Only the concluding pages are reproduced here.)

---

1. This word which is used more and more often, describes both an economic and social reality that coincides with a growing awareness. It should however not be misleading: the world has not become a uniform plane, where all relations are correlations. Hierarchies still exist, break down and are reconstructed according to different planes, other boundaries, and other lines. We therefore use the word "interdependence" in its broader sense, and without claiming to erase the differences – on the contrary.

The transfer of sovereignty that should result from the creation of a European central bank worthy of the name will authorize a totally new kind of event. For the first time ever, a community of nations will have decided to go beyond itself to attain a superior state. No doubt there is a similar case in past history, that of the United States, but never will century-old states (England, Spain and France, to take the oldest ones) have banded together to the point of limiting their own power in order to give themselves collective power. Much more than an alliance or multilateral agreement is involved, as was the case, for example, with the various international monetary agreements throughout the twentieth century. What we have here is a genuine transformation of "singular societies" into an "objectivized social universal". The form in which a European central bank is to be constituted bears witness to this.

It is quite close to what happened in the setting up of national central banks in individual countries. Not until the end of the seventeenth century do we find the first central banks, the Bank of Stockholm (1668) and, especially, the Bank of England (1694). Although publicly capitalized banks had existed before this (in particular in Genoa, but also, as we know with certainty, in ancient Egypt and Greece), the birth of the Bank of England marks a turning point in the history of capitalism and modern society[2]. Until then it had been indispensable to back all monetary symbols with a tangible reality, gold or silver; it was henceforth possible to guarantee these symbols with a simple public signature. There was not a brutal change, but rather a slow development in which a system based on Nature gradually turned into a system founded on institutions. The central bank led human society into a new stage of its history: it assured the juncture between two financial circuits, that of royal power and that of the community.

All financial activity would now be re-organized around an institution whose name indicates its two-fold nature: as a bank, it is part of the economy and deals essentially with monetary affairs; as central, it relates to political power and guarantees the permanence of the entire financial system. "I will help you, I will save you, but I will enslave you", wrote Fernand Braudel regarding this kind of institution[3]. This twofold nature of the central bank can be observed in all countries that have one, that is, almost all countries in the world.

There has been strong debate over the last two centuries about whether the central bank should be independent of the political authorities or not. In the nineteenth century, an economist

2. Concerning this, see our book, *Que l'argent soit – capitalisme et alchimie de l'avenir*, Calmann-Lévy, 1993, especially chapter IX.

3. Fernand Braudel, *Civilisation matérielle, Économie et capitalisme, XVe-XVIIIe siècle*, tome III, chapitre IV, Armand Colin, 1980, p. 251.

named Ricardo maintained that leaving the government total latitude in the matter of monetary creation presented great dangers, such as that of the absence of limits to the creation of money by the government. Ricardo wrote: "Experience shows that whenever a government or bank has had an unlimited faculty to emit paper money, it has always abused it[4]." We need only replace "paper money" by "credit" to describe a major contemporary worry.

In any event, the issue of the independence of monetary power has been raised: should a central bank be independent or not? In some countries, such as Great Britain or Japan, there is no independence, in others, like Germany or the United States, there is a high degree of independence, often linked to the legal status of the governor of the bank (who names and removes him). This difference does not mean that in one case the external value of the money (the exchange rate) is unstable or weak, while in the other it is stable or strong. The stability of a currency depends on various related factors, such as the strength of the national economy, the interest rates, the political climate, the "memory" of international capital markets, the judgement of experts, the global image of how the institutions function, etc. But the fact is that in the framework of Europe a consensus has formed in favour of the independence of the future European central bank. It should be noted, however, that the absolute independence of a central bank would be a contradiction in terms.

Central banks were created in part because merchants and other agents of economic activity regularly saw their need for monetary liquidity increase, while the gold and silver mines could not satisfy this need. On the one hand there was the ruler (a sovereign prince) who disposed of precious metal that he intended to coin as he pleased, on the other there was the community, monetarily dependent, which had always done what it could to protect itself against royal whim and fluctuations of supply, and which consistently tried to reduce its quantitative dependence. In line with the remarks such people as William Petty, it was soon understood that the shortage of money called for currency creation that did not totally depend on nature's generosity. This gave rise to institutions having the power to create money, also called institutions of emission. In other words, central banks were invented to reduce man's dependence on nature. How, then, can it logically be maintained that societies that have given themselves such instruments should renounce them in the name of the proper management of their currency? In fact two principles must be reaffirmed that are not contradictory, but quite complementary: monetary management

---

4. David Ricardo, *Principles of political economy and taxation*, coll. « Champs », Flammarion, 1981, p. 316.

should be handled autonomously by a central bank, but this bank should be entrusted with a mission for which it is to be held accountable. A central bank should, therefore, be at once dependent and autonomous. This should also be the case with the European central bank, to be created before the end of the century.

On a different level, we find here a debate that was motivated by reflections of postmodern philosophy: since independence can lead us to forget about others, autonomy must adopt two principles: the assertion of the subject and the recognition of the other as the very basis of this assertion. Marc-Alain Ouaknin notes, in this respect: "A fundamental observation: autonomy is not a freedom without rules. In the ideal of autonomy, man remains dependent on norms and laws, provided that he accepts them freely[5]". The basic idea is the same, transposed to the level of states and the institutions they have in common.

The analogy with the movement described by Hegel in his *Principles* is striking, even if it is audacious to transpose the relation individual/society to the relation single society/community of societies. In fact, this is a "modern" dimension that we find in certain philosophical thinking. We have in mind here what Apel has written: "In the present world situation where, for the first time, different civilizations and forms of existence must cohabit and work together in an order of planetary peace, one must radically modify a pluralist ethics of values to an axiologically universalist ethics: as Kant had foreseen, the search for happiness – in other words the individual's assumption of himself in the sense of a good life and the corresponding choice of supreme values – must be abandoned in great measure to each particular individual and to each particular form of existence. But at the same time, we should continue to want these norms, whose function is to regulate life in common – and, beyond this, work in common, with coresponsibility, towards resolving the problems faced by mankind – to be recognized by all as universally valid and obligatory. And yet these universally valid norms, such as the equality of all before the law and the coresponsibility of all, cannot but constrict, at all times, the field in which the different evaluations operate, in that they concern the individual's assumption of himself (the "concern for oneself") of which Foucault speaks[6]".

This text is remarkable in that it clearly raises the question arising from postmodernity. The answer is also clear: "The

5. Marc-Alain Ouaknin, *Méditations érotiques, Essai sur Emmanuel Lévinas*, Balland, 1992, p. 122.
6. K.O. Apel, "Une éthique universaliste est-elle possible?", in *La philosophie en Europe*, Raymond Klibanski et David Pears (dir.), Folio Gallimard with the assistance of UNESCO, 1993, p. 501-502.

ethics of discussion ... as an ethics of the consensus formed by communication, undertakes the moral task of mediating by communication between the universal norms of deontological ethics and the evaluations – no doubt incommensurable – of the individual's assumption of himself in the diverse forms of existence'". Apel adds: "I defend ... the opinion that, if this unity of humanity and its history in the eighteenth century was only a vision of European philosophers, it has become today an irreversible technical, economic, political, and ecological reality. Consequently, it should also – as solidarity in coresponsibility – become a moral reality[8]".

Thus the question of intersubjective dialogue arises: does it transcend the national communities formed of citizens, establishing a sort of transnational intersubjectivity that overflows state borders, or should it be restricted to inter-individual relations, and inspire only via its dialectics the relations between communities?

---

7. K.O. Apel, "Une éthique universaliste est-elle possible?", *op. cit.*, p. 503.
8. *Ibidem*, p.504.

Ex-socialist Europe

Stéphane Douailler

This study begins with the viewpoint that the aim of the survey "Philosophy and democracy in the word" is to examine the present development of certain features common to the history of philosophy teachers and the democratic idea, a history that seems to be highly variable in the democratization process of central Europe.

Is the idea that there is a common situation shared by the former Socialist countries of Europe in the areas of philosophy and democracy an illusion? Are, perhaps, the different traditions, differing in periods of time, states of fragmentation, degrees of effectiveness, that might serve as inspiration for the democratic use of philosophical education, so varied that the different countries that have emerged from ex-socialist Europe are being led along different paths, especially in the immediate future? In fact, even if the idea of democracy and the diversity of circumstances are not the only factors, does recent history not show just such fragmentation?

Nevertheless, the immediate future of these countries is one in which what is in some respects a common history is still visible, linking them to one another in a way that is far from superficial. They are not, to be sure, the only countries to have been involved in the enterprise of building socialism in a single country, whose effects were world-wide. But, while they were affected in different ways, they were directly integrated in this process, over many years, and together lived through its collapse. In spite of its real diversity this period was a shared experience, if not all the time, at least at certain critical instants, including the moment of the collapse.

The collapse does have certain features of a democratic episode. It is in fact, even if its meaning is far from being immediately graspable, even if it still remains quite difficult to understand, even if the issue of democracy often arose in non-operational ways, a democratic episode shared by the members of Ex-socialist Europe. It probably still remains so, not in a general but in a real sense, and will as long as, among a number of other factors, this episode itself gives the issue a certain urgency and weight in the formulation of new conditions for the exercise and teaching of philosophy. For it was not at all obvious that the political collapse of ex-socialist Europe would spare and even renew the desire to teach philosophy. As Professor Edouard Swiderski, of the Eastern European Institute of the University of Freiburg[1] has written, in his 1993 article "The crisis of continuity in post-soviet Russian philosophy[2]", at the moment of the cultural crisis caused by perestroïka, the question of philosophy was raised both with respect to doubts about the institution of philosophy as is, about its viability, and with respect to its elimination. Thus the forms in which philosophical education is, more or less vigorously, being rethought in the ex-socialist countries of Europe, involve, in part, decisions related to the collapse of the system to which they belonged, which included a certain type of philosophical instruction. In this regard the decisions being taken with respect to the teaching of philosophy can be understood as proposed practical interpretations of the European democracy emerging from this collapse.

The relation between the previous official philosophy and the clandestine philosophy is then analyzed, and the idea of a philosophical renaissance and its diverse forms is described. The following are the last pages of the article.

And, in the final analysis, we are perhaps led to reject, two pictures of philosophy in ex-Socialist Europe, one which sees genuine philosophy as having a totally clandestine history, a pure matter of work done in the catacombs, hidden in the crevices of civil society or private life, a totally secret continuation of thought during the years of triumphant official Marxism, and another picture which simply sees this history as fragmented, with each doing his job as a philosopher and where, in a political period which was singularly difficult and diversely evaluable, in which philosophy had to be reborn, each worker, in his own way, in a variety of different forms, made his own contribution. What such pictures should not let us lose sight of is the true obscurity of the situation, what should not be forgotten is what in fact identifies a philosophical journey, for example sincerity, courage, and the joy of victory.

Making teaching philosophical

In fact it is never evident anywhere what is and is not philosophy. In particular, one cannot simply take the most powerful states of the western world as the contemporary reality and the

1. University of Freiburg, Eastern European Institute, "Studies in East European Thought", Portes de Fribourg, 1763, Granges-Pacot, Switzerland.
2. E. M. Swiderski, "The Crisis of continuity in Post-soviet Russian Philosophy", in *Philosophy and Political Change in Eastern Europe*, ed. by Barry Smith, La Salle, Illinois, 1993.

model for a new Greece. Nietzsche's *Schopenhauer als Erzieher* (*Schopenhauer as educator*, 1874), for example, stated this about philosophy at the very time Germany had the most renowned chairs of philosophy. And he showed that philosophy was also, in this situation, in danger of non-existence. It is no doubt a good thing that Estonia has turned toward the experience of the Scandinavian countries[3], that Latvia has revived the tradition of the Herder Institute of Riga, inviting as much as a third of its associated professors from Germany, the United States or Denmark[4], that Bulgarian[5], Croatian[6], Hungarian[7], Slovene[8], Slovak[9], Czech[10] professors are translating Maria Fürst's *Einführung in die Philosophie*, A. Azanbacher's *Einleitung in die Philosophie*, or Harry Stottlemeir's *Discovery*, that the significant works of the last few decades are hastily being published, that the University of Moscow invites French and German speakers who are likely to provoke animated discussions[11]. But, to take the last example, the spectacle of these evenings of strong intellectual confrontation, as described by a Moscow university member, in which she tells of her enthusiasm at discovering the virtues of free thinking and pluralism, has a negative side. For those who describe these encounters for a survey conducted by UNESCO in 1993, who paint the Russian university growing from the collapse as a joyous profusion of intellectual activities, of happy confidence in the conceptions of the world offered by the plurality of philosophies, of a proud commitment to philosophical reason alongside life threatened by the age of technology, give a picture in which no doubt Western powers would be quite happy to recognize themselves. But in such a picture, apparently, what is beginning to fade, has perhaps already been lost, is the courage to despair of ever finding the truth, the triumphant joy of obeying a deep-felt need, which, according to Nietzsche, marks the true path of philosophy in a world in which it is an obscure question. And under such

3. Rein Ruutsoo, "Teaching philosophy in Estonia", p. 10.
4. Uldis Suna, "Latvia", p. 12.
5. Aneta Karageorgieva, "Philosophy classes in Bulgarian Schools", *Europa forum philosophie*, n° 28, april 1993, p. 28.
6. Miljenko Brkic, "Philosophieunterricht in Kroatien", p. 15.
7. Eva Gabor, "Der Philosophieunterricht in Ungarn seit September 1993", *Europa forum philosophie*, n° 31, october 1994, p. 8.
8. Marjan Simenc, "Teaching philosophy in Slovenia", p. 19.
9. Ladislav Kiczko, "Philosophieunterricht an der Mittelschulen der Slowakei", *Europa forum philosophie*, n° 29, october 1993, p. 17.
10. Jaroslava Schlegelová, "Die Situation in der tschechischen Republik", *Europa forum philosophie*, n° 28, april 1993, p. 20.
11. T. I. Oizerman et S.T. Melioukhine, "Russie, les années 1990", p. 420.

conditions it is certainly not philosophy in its uniqueness that is concerned by this desire to evoke and mimic for us a public space in the university where it is now supposed to have found its home. The manifestations of a thirst for multiplying points of view, distinguishing positions, pursuing dialogue, diversifying or intensifying a republic of discussion, do not provide a locus for philosophical questioning, which must continue to seek its own way. On the other hand, such manifestations have much to do with the idea of democracy. And if they choose here and there to occupy the spaces of philosophical activity for no immediately evident philosophical reason, this choice nevertheless always has a historical basis in a past or present association of philosophy and democratic episodes. Characteristic features of this history were manifest in ex-Socialist Europe, when, for example, 46,000 copies of the *Philosophical works* of Alfred North Whitehead were sold in Russia[12] in 1990, or, even more astonishingly, when in 1982 in Lithuania (a country with a population of about 3.6 million) five thousand copies of Kant's *Critique of Pure Reason*[13] were snapped up in one week. With this sort of thing happening, one of the responses apparently to be expected from both countries and philosophers is that they are to try to think as deeply as possible about the teaching of philosophy. The situation, for reasons which perhaps cannot be elucidated, but which history keeps bringing up, would require not so much a response to an apparent demand for a philosophical content of the idea of democracy, but rather to think thoroughly about that courses of study, textbooks programmes, and methods which can give a resolutely philosophical sense to the teaching of philosophy in a democratic educational system.

12. T. A. Alekseeva, "Russie, les contacts actuels avec les traditions occidentales", p. 427.
13. Tomas Sodeika, "Wozu philosophische Texte ins Litauische übersetzen? (metaphysisch gefragt)", *Europa forum Philosophie*, n° 31, october 1994, p. 14.

II

A DOUBLE POSITION

> *"You wouldn't believe, gentlemen, how diffi-*
> *cult it is to get rid of philosophy. Not to philo-*
> *sophize is still to philosophize, but without*
> *method, with a sort of naive brutality."*
> Gabriel Séailles, 1904.

Overview

Is it desirable to extend the place of philosophical reflection in education? If so, how? By multiplying philosophy departments in universities? By adding new courses in most higher education programmes? Through an initiation to philosophy at the secondary level? If so, should this be given only in the last year of school or earlier, and at what age?

Whatever the answer, how is it to be justified? In the name of what should we prefer to restrict the teaching of philosophy, or refuse a proposed extension? For what reasons, on the contrary, would we want to develop it, but limit it only to universities? What reasons would be put forward by the partisans of the introduction of philosophy at the end of secondary studies? Need we really oppose those who believe that only the last year should include instruction in philosophy to those who have chosen systems where the initiation to philosophy is spread over the last two or three years of secondary education?

In fact, should we confine philosophical education to school systems alone? Why limit this time of reflection to adolescence and the first years of adult life? The questions philosophy asks continue to be relevant during our whole existence. They will even be understood, in general, more richly with the increasing experience of life and its different situations. Might we not imagine giving adults opportunities to learn about philosophy, beyond the years in which the young are usually educated? Why are such initiatives not part of the project of permanent education open to all?

Issues such as these are raised in the replies to the UNESCO survey cited in the following pages. It might be thought that everything opposes the multiple viewpoints expressed. The diversity of national legislation, cultural practices, and the interpretation of the key words of each question could lead to an indefinite fragmentation. The disparity of situation and language could have been such that any attempt to compare them was doomed from the start.

But this is not the case. Two major poles or points of view can be clearly discerned. Each of these involves a way of envisaging the relation between philosophy and democracy. Let us try to describe them briefly. They define what might be called the "double position" of the place of philosophy in the world.

According to first point of view, philosophy and democracy are considered as separate elements, developing independently, neither interacting with the other. Philosophy is a specialized discipline among others, and judged to be accessible only to a small number. Overall, it is considered to resemble certain branches of mathematics or physics, which can be approached only by a few, because of their high level of abstraction, the long training period required, the rare aptitudes demanded, the limited attraction they have for most people. Seen as identical in this respect to scientific research, philosophy's major distinctive feature seems to be that of having no practical application at all. Its apparent useless makes it an enigma for the general public. All this does not argue in favour of extending of the teaching of a subject which, according to this point of view, is reserved by definition to a few university departments.

In spite of everything, it is not the specialization of research or the difficulty due to its abstraction that keep philosophy out of the general curriculum. After all mathematics are taught, in its simpler forms and then with increasing difficulty, at all levels. It is almost unanimously judged that this subject provides good intellectual training, even if the rudiments of algebra and geometry acquired in youth rarely, if ever, prove useful later on. Philosophical analyses are not viewed in the same way. They are not seen as something it is necessary to know something about. The mind can pursue its growth, completely and harmoniously, even if no philosophical dimension is an explicit part of its training.

One fundamental point dominates this first view: political education is carried out elsewhere and otherwise, than in philosophy classes. No political role is recognized for this teaching. Nothing in its nature is judged to be indispensable to civic life and the forming of the citizen. This is not necessarily a deprecatory judgment: the importance of philosophy is not denied in general. But it is not granted at all for general education. This is worth insisting on: it is important not to confuse this absence of philosophy in the secondary educational system with a disavowal of philosophy as such, or even with a lack of interest for the philosophical approach to the problems raised by the organization of political life. "Political philosophy" as an area of research and university teaching might very well be encouraged by the university and by the State, but the political dimension of "general philosophy" might still be considered unimportant.

The idea that the reading of Plato or Aristotle, Descartes or Spinoza, Hume or Kant, Leibniz or Hegel might make an essential, or even irreplaceable, contribution to the education of most people is simply non-existent. Such an idea is more or less unthinkable from this viewpoint. To repeat, this is not because the difficulty of the texts involved does not allow widespread diffusion. It is because philosophical reflection itself, whether or not it is stripped of its historical references or scholarly vocabulary, does not seem to be a relevant model for "learning about freedom".

According to this first point of view, either freedom is not something that has to be "learned", for it is entirely present from the start, without having to be discovered, or else it is acquired elsewhere and otherwise. At the secondary level, it can be through the study of literature, history, or scientific methodology, for example, that the capacities and limits of the mind will be discovered. Outside of school, religious practice, family education, political activities, professional life, sports, etc. contribute to the education of responsible and free individuals. Philosophical reflection is not supposed to be part of this, either as a social reality or as a educational ideal.

This first possibility can be seen, more or less clearly delineated, in the various conceptions of the place and role of philosophical instruction to be found in the English-speaking countries and those influenced by the anglo-saxon educational system. The opposite pole corresponds to French-speaking countries and those of Latin culture. The diversity of national situations obviously introduces many differences in the actual cases. It is nevertheless possible to sketch the basic outline of this other way of viewing the place of philosophy in education and in democracy.

According to the second point of view, philosophy teaching is an integral part of the realization of the democratic ideal. Not only are philosophy and democracy not considered to be dissociated in their development and objectives, but learning to think philosophically is conceived of as a vital element of the training of citizens. This is why it is given a place at the end of secondary studies. Nothing, basically, would rule out starting an initiation to philosophy even earlier. A certain level of instruction is necessary, most often, for the child to have the concepts needed for a minimal understanding of philosophical interrogations. But this is not a reason to subordinate the practice of philosophical reflection to the preceding mastery of a large body of different kinds of knowledge.

For, viewed this way, philosophy is not a rare speciali-zation. It can be, and should be, everyone's concern. This is how it participates directly in the construction of democracy. The exercise of philosophical thinking is no longer to be conceived as an approach to the history of ideas or the pursuit of logical analysis. It must first of all help each individual to practice analyzing of his or her own convictions, to grasp the diversity of arguments and viewpoints of others, to perceive the limited nature of even our surest knowledge. In that, it is indeed a teaching addressed to all. It should contribute to developing the judgmental capacities of citizens, fundamental for democracy.

It is clear that this is a point of principle. No-one would maintain that only those who have been initiated to philosophical thinking are well trained and fully free citizens! Such a position would mean that the vast majority, who have not had access to philosophical instruction during their school years, would be intellectually and morally handicapped and politically underdeveloped. Must we wait, for full democracy to appear, until all citizens have received such instruction? This would obviously be an excessive and untenable conclusion!

But the really important point, here, is the claim that there is a continuous relation between philosophy and democracy. The extension of philosophy teaching is considered *ipso facto* to be an extension of democracy. If this was not so, then in a sense philosophy would be untrue to itself. While this is not always totally explicit, it must be supposed, for such a point of view to be possible and coherent, that the universality of reason, which is the basis of the philosophical act, and legal and political equality, which are the conditions of democracy, are fundamentally alike in nature. At least, we must assume that they are united by ties so powerful that each reinforces the advancement of the other. On this initial conception depend a whole series of consequences, which concern not only the existence of philosophy teaching at the end of secondary school, but the fact that this instruction is compulsory, that philosophy is an examination subject, that its programmes are developed by the State, etc.

Between these two poles, as we shall see, there are many more small differences, and a few hybrids. But it does not seem possible, in the actual state of world cultures, to distinguish a third basic position. These two main possibilities determine the very sense given to philosophy teaching and the question of its extension, and also the significance of philosophy teaching aimed at adults. The replies to the survey give further detail, and sometimes complicate, these preliminary indications of the "double position" of philosophy.

Data from the survey

The table at the end of the volume collects the answers to the question "Is philosophy a special subject at the secondary level?" This table speaks for itself, so little comment is needed. Firstly, it is easy to see that the number of countries where such teaching exists is very much higher than is generally believed. It is generally known that philosophy teaching exists in the final secondary school years in certain European countries (France, Italy, Portugal) or Latin America (Chile, Peru), and Africa (Benin, Mali, Senegal). The general impression, if one does not have a wide enough range of data, is that these are exceptions, particular cases, almost oddities. But a world-wide perspective, even partial, greatly changes this picture.

We see that many other countries must be added to the few mentioned above. First, countries of central Europe. Often backed by a rich philosophical tradition, they are now in a situation in which there is resonance between philosophy teaching in secondary schools and the democratization of political and social life. This is the case, for example, in Bulgaria. Ivan Kolev, assistant professor at the University of Sofia St. Clement of Ohrid, co-author of new programmes and new manuals of philosophy, notes that "in the universities, the teaching of philosophy has a certain lack of favour, while in the secondary schools its prestige is increasing". This is also the case in Romania, where philosophy has always figured in secondary school programmes, but where, as Professor Petru Ioan writes, "since the changes of 1989, the teaching of the humanities in general, and philosophy in particular, has seen remarkable growth, as witnessed by the continued increase in the number of candidates." In his eyes, this "dynamic of the interest for philosophy teaching" corresponds to the evolution of the world, to the "emergence of forces calling for an open society".

This is also the case with Albania, discussed in the preceding chapter, and Croatia, where philosophy is taught, according to the reply of the Institute of Philosophy of the University of Zagreb, in the form of courses in logic and the history of philosophy, at the end of secondary school. In Slovakia, an initiation to philosophy and its history is also an integral part of the last year of secondary education, and this is also the case in the Czech Republic, where, in the same curriculum, courses are taught on the basics of ethics, the theory of knowledge and the history of philosophy.

Thus such courses also exist in very different countries of Europe, with, sometimes, early opportunities for learning about philosophical reflection. In Finland, for example, in addition to compulsory courses at the end of secondary education, younger students (age 13-15) can choose an initiation to philosophy as an option. In Greece, the teaching of philosophy is part of the programme of the last three years of secondary school. The course begins with selected passages in the writings of Plato and Aristotle, and does not last the whole of the first year. In the following two years, there is systematic instruction in history of philosophy, ethics, theory of knowledge, and logic. In Turkey, since 1992-93, two introductory courses are compulsory, and two others ("Philosophical Texts" and "History of Philosophy") are offered as options. Logic is taught as a separate course, and ethics as part of a programme entitled "Religious and Ethical Culture".

In Africa, those States influenced by the French model (Benin, Cameroon, Ivory Coast, Mali, Senegal, among others) have kept philosophy teaching in the last year of secondary school, and in many cases have renovated it. Some States have even extended it to the last two or three years of secondary school. Thus, in Benin, philosophy has been taught in the last three years of secondary school for the past ten years. In the Ivory Coast, in the 1980's philosophy courses were introduced "as an experiment" in the next-to-last year of secondary education.

Other countries where the French influence was important have extended philosophy, by creating courses that start earlier in the school curriculum, at least in certain programmes. Thus, in Morocco, "philosophy is taught in the options Modern Literature and Original Literature in the last two years of secondary education and in the options Experimental Sciences, Mathematics, and Economic Sciences and Techniques in the last year of secondary education". In Tunisia, the educational reform of 1988 introduced the teaching of philosophy "in the year just before the final year in the Literature course".

Although this type of extension is relatively rare at the secondary level, it can be asked how much it might prefigure, in countries influenced by the French model, the creation of a system which is inspired both by this historical heritage and the model of an initiation to philosophy normally spread over more than a single year, found in Portugal, for example, where "philosophy is a compulsory subject in the general curriculum of all the courses in the tenth and eleventh years of school".

Such a gradual initiation, spread over the last few years of secondary education, is particularly common in Latin America. Thus, in Uruguay, as the reply of Professor Mauricio Langon, Inspector, indicates, philosophy teaching has, since the last century, been part of the secondary curriculum, and has recently been extended to professional technical education. At present, all sections receive, in the final three years, three hours of philosophy courses per week.

Another way to extend philosophical instruction, when it is already present at the secondary level, is to make it compulsory where it is only optional. This is the current situation in Brazil, where the matter is under discussion. According to the reply from the professors of the Rio Grande do Sul University, "there is general agreement to return to the compulsory teaching of philosophy at the secondary level. We are also asking whether this subject should be more common in all secondary curricula in schools where it is now taught only in one or two sections." The four authors of the response from the philosophy department of the University of Brasilia indicate, on this point, that "some argue for an increase in the number of hours devoted to philosophy, considering that it improves students' critical sense and develops their reasoning capacities, while their opponents would prefer to strengthen the teaching of mathematics or Portuguese".

It might seem a simple matter to determine whether philosophy is taught, in the form of optional or compulsory courses, at the secondary level, the question requiring no more than a simple "yes" or "no" answer. But this is not always the case. In Cuba, for instance, the teaching of philosophy is not part of the curriculum of secondary level students. However, as Professor Juan Mari Lois of the Felix Varela Centre notes, in the programme for the ninth year of secondary education there was, a few years ago, a course on the "Fundamentals of political knowledge" which included a great deal of philosophy. This course has been replaced by a programme of civic education which "is more a programme of ethics than a programme of philosophy proper, since it deals with philosophy from the standpoint of one of its components, ethics, while also treating other subjects which are not strictly philosophical." In pre-university courses, a programme devoted to the "Foundations of Marxism-Leninism" could inspire similar remarks.

Along the same lines, the reply from China raises questions. It states that "at the secondary level, philosophy is a separate subject". The courses deal with "the basic topics of philosophy (dialectic materialism and historical materialism), the history of the development of societies and the vision of man". The question that can be raised is not: "can the teaching of Marxism-Leninism as such be considered to be philosophical instruction?" but rather: "can teaching from an *exclusively* Marxist viewpoint be philosophical?" Not, let us repeat, because it is Marxist, but because it presents itself as the unique possessor of the truth. The pluralism which basically defines democracy also defines philosophical education. But should we then conclude that eclecticism, relativism or scepticism should reign in philosophy? Of course not, if we really believe that truth is unique. But each person should be able to seek it among many possibilities made equally available.

This equality should apply to Marxism itself. It is often believed, by those mistakenly confusing it with the official ideologies that proclaimed it, that Marxism disappeared as a theory with the collapse of many communist states. But this is incorrect. The intellectual scope of the concepts and approach of Marx remains powerful. What has harmed it is the exclusive domination exercised by a simplified, dogmatic doctrine, whose actual application was in general far from either philosophy or democracy.

The recent past can have unexpected consequences for the attitude towards philosophy and the extension of its teaching. In situations where this teaching is too strongly marked by Marxism, because the same teachers are still there, some people propose reducing philosophy teaching in order to develop democracy! This is what Professor Dobrokhotov of the University of Moscow describes: "It has been claimed that it is appropriate to temporarily reduce the place of philosophy in higher education. This is generally the argument of democrats, uneasy about the place occupied, in the teaching of philosophy at present, by a dogmatism and scholasticism which it is impossible to eliminate by administrative methods."

The opposite standpoint, that in which training for citizenship is to be undertaken totally independently of any philosophy teaching, is represented perfectly by the judgment of Professor Michael Dummett, of Oxford University: "It is essential that some should study philosophy. But I doubt that this study can be judged to be essential for most individuals." Whereas, from the preceding perspective, this "essential" character seemed evident, here it is at best uncertain. "I think that the teaching of philosophy is essential for dealing with today's social, technological and international transformations, but this point of view is not widespread in my country, which tends to consider philosophy as quite old-fashioned, inefficient, and scholastic", writes Professor Richard Shusterman of Temple University, in the USA.

The question of the "popularity" of philosophy should be mentioned, since to ask if philosophy should have a greater place than it does at present is also to try to determine how much favour it appears to have with students, and perhaps also with the general public. It would be artificial, and ultimately a waste of time, to willfully increase the time devoted to a discipline which does not fulfil anybody's expectations.

Does philosophy interest people? More than it did ten or twenty years ago? It is obviously impossible to formulate a world-wide answer to such questions. Simply aligning "yes" and "no" answers would make little sense. Statistically, we may note that the increase in enthusiasm wins out over the pattern of a decline. But, on this matter, the explanations, arguments, and comments are more interesting and more revealing than the statistics.

Among the motives invoked to explain a relative lack of interest is an excess of schooling. For instance, the reply from Morocco states that "while it had been perceived as an awakening of the mind to intellectual autonomy, philosophy teaching is now only seen as a set of ideas to be memorized for examinations." In many other countries, it is the absence of competent instructors which is said to explain the decline of philosophy teaching. "In Russia, most teachers of philosophy are marked by the old system, their professional level is not very high, and their attachment to democratic ideals is purely verbal", states Professor Dobrokhotov of the University of Moscow. The lack of favour for philosophy teaching can also be attributed "to religious causes in general", as the reply from Qatar indicates, or to political causes, as the reply from Slovakia indicates: "Philosophy has lost credit because, under the communist regime, it had become an instrument of totalitarianism."

One possible cause of decline is mentioned more frequently than all the rest: the absence of any economic and social benefit from philosophical training. The world crisis has made it necessary to favour courses of study leading to a job. The reply from Slovakia states that "philosophy is considered to be a luxury". On this point, judgments from all over the world converge. Here are comments that sound almost like news flashes from very different countries. Zaire: "In public opinion, to study philosophy, or the humanities in general, is to condemn oneself to unemployment." Australia: "Political pressure from Camberra in the eighties to make universities 'more efficient' has not strengthened philosophy." The Dominican Republic: "A professional philosopher is considered a Don Quixote." From the United Kingdom: "A degree in philosophy is not a job qualification." In short, in a society that is governed around the world by the requirements of technology, philosophical instruction might seem more likely to decline than to grow.

However, its demise is not predicted. Even those who note its relative lack of favour emphasize its essentialness. The reply from Morocco is categorical: "More than indispensable, this subject is vital, in the strongest sense of the term. The world at present is undergoing swift and simultaneous changes. If citizens do not have an intellectual tool for integration that is very powerful and polyvalent (philosophy), the forces acting on our world will push them toward the path of disintegration. Knowing how to philosophize develops a form of intellectual immunity against particularistic reductions."

The fact that philosophy does not create jobs does not prevent it from continuing to be attractive. It would seem as if the same world-wide technological system both hinders and requires philosophical reflection. As the reply from Norway stresses, "there is a strong interest in ethics which doubtless reflects the problems of modern society: distributive justice, the control of technology (genetic engineering) and environmental issues. Political circles seem to consider these philosophical questions legitimate to a greater extent than previously."

Not only is philosophy not judged to be dead, or dying, but the future relations between its reflexive mode of existence and this technologized world, in which we all live to a greater or lesser extent, are frequently presented with enthusiasm and passion. The unique, almost "redemptive", character of philosophical thought is often emphasized. According to the reply from the philosophy department of the University of Brasilia, "different sources agree that only philosophy can furnish the critical tool to demystify the presuppositions and effects of technology and the political statements and projects inspired by it". The reply from the University of Hacettepe (Ankara, Turkey) considers that philosophy constitutes "perhaps the most essential human attempt to counter the principle that 'anything goes' and the supposed equality of all values and norms". As Professor Mauricio Langon (Uruguay) writes, such reflection is "particularly indispensable in an age when the technical power available to mankind is a real power to destroy others, our own planet, and ourselves. To train men and women to be ready to deal with the challenges of the twenty-first century is not possible without philosophy".

A first analysis

Must we choose between training people and causing them to be unemployed? This is simply the wrong way to formulate the problem. Let us try to see it a little more clearly.

In order to avoid confusion, it is absolutely necessary to stop opposing scientific, technical and professional training, on the one hand, and philosophy teaching, on the other. We must keep the different functions apart. In secondary education, the role of philosophy is not to turn students into qualified philosophers able to teach or do research themselves. In higher education, *only* the programmes for students specializing in philosophy and taking specific degrees prepare the way to professional opportunities.

All higher study programmes should be able to include philosophy courses adapted to their particular needs. These courses should not be considered as external elements of these professional and technical subjects, but on the contrary, should be fully integrated. Instead of being seen as stealing time that could be devoted to more serious and profitable subjects, they should be viewed as an essential part of the assimilation of these subjects.

Let us hammer the point. The value philosophy adds is not the job opportunities it offers. It is the possibility of a new perspective on the subject being studied. It is the new understanding of local techniques that is given by broader interrogations. It is the sharing of the intellectual perplexities and subtleties which make us human.

This will not convince the doubters. They will argue that programmes everywhere are getting heavier and heavier, that hours of study are increasing and getting harder to organize. Under such conditions, why give even a small part of this precious time to issues which, while perhaps interesting, are always *less* useful, directly and practically, than more technical training?

This is an old debate. We might mockingly put this last objection as: why reflect, when there is so much to do? Why try to understand, when there is so much to learn? Why think, instead of doing? It is true that the domination of technique leads to such forms of behaviour. It is true that it makes the non-human possible. But it would be a mistake to exaggerate and shout about this. Social situations are constraining, and sometimes cruel. They explain why we often give our preference to immediate efficacy.

All we need do is make it clear that time given to philosophy is not wasted. Many authors have already done this. Among them, Gabriel Séailles at the beginning of the century, listed the essential points it is useful to recall here. He was professor of philosophy at the Sorbonne in Paris, and contributed to the founding of the Ligue des droits de l'homme and "popular universities". His text remains sufficiently relevant to need no comment. It comes from *L'enseignement secondaire et la philosophie* (1904).

"Do you think that a year is lost when it is spent teaching young men that first appearances do not reveal all of truth? Do you think that is not a good thing that for his reflections on human nature, on his needs and the reasons for his beliefs, on science and morals, he should be informed that all is not clear, that the world and thought pose complex problems that must be approached with modesty? In a society as divided as ours, tolerance is a necessary virtue: in revealing the mind to itself, we extend it, broaden it, augment it, humanize it. We cannot reduce foolishness without reducing evil a little. We have the right to expect from philosophical instruction not the contemptuous indifference, the ironic pity of the skeptic for the believer, nor even that tolerance of the religious man which is merely the reaction of charity, 'always kind, always patient', towards those who are haughtily convinced of possessing and offering absolute truth, but that respect for the beliefs of others that is inspired by our awareness of the moral effort, conspired to by the soul in its entirety, by which we have created and maintain our own convictions."

Let us not forget that these convictions about the role of philosophical education are far from being shared by all. As we have already observed, philosophy has a double position. It can be specialized academic research, or an educational discipline directed to all. These two poles can be separate or connected. One can be favoured to the detriment of the other. We must try to develop them jointly, as far as this is possible in the diverse traditions that exist.

For it would be futile to try to rid philosophy of this double nature. Going beyond specific cultural traditions, it is no doubt one of the most fundamental traits of philosophy. Its doubleness corresponds not only to the distinction between higher and secondary education, or that between a discipline for specialists and a training for freedom. Between the education of the young and of adults philosophy has, again, a double nature. But also between books and life; between knowledge and ignorance; between the singularity of the self and the universality of ideas. And also between politics in the narrow sense and politics in the broad sense. This last point deserves elucidation. It is the next finding of this survey.

PHILOSOPHY AND DEMOCRACY IN THE UNITED STATES
Christian Delacampagne

The study analyzes the specific relationship between philosophy and religion in the United States, the domination of analytic philosophy in academia and its recent development, and the place of philosophy in social and political conflicts. Here is the end of the article.

Do American "intellectuals" exist?

In this form, the question may seem ironic, if not ill-intentioned. But it is not meant to be, for what is intended is not the most current sense of the word "intellectual", but rather a historical-cultural sense. In the usual sense, an intellectual is someone who exercises a professional activity, literary or academic, or who has this kind of cultural baggage; in this sense, many Americans are intellectuals.

There exists, however, a historical model of the intellectual specifically linked to European culture and in particular to French culture: in this sense the intellectual is a philosopher, or a writer interested in philosophy, who conceives his task as a social mission, and intervenes frequently in debates of general interest, not just for the pleasure of expressing his opinion but primarily in order to influence that of the general public, and so contribute to the development of society. Bertrand Russell in Great Britain, and Voltaire, Hugo, Sartre and Aron in France, were intellectuals of this type.

But curiously, this classical type in the history of ideas in Europe seems strangely absent from the American tradition. It may be useful to ask why.

The first explanation that comes to mind is the highly specialized conception that academics in the United States have of philosophy, and the way they teach it. Not only is philosophy for them a technical discipline, whose complexity makes it difficult to communicate to the general public, but, in addition, the domains in which it is most often exercized – the analysis of scientific language, reflection on the functioning of knowledge – are quite far removed from any social or political preoccupations.

A second reason, symmetrical to the first, involves the lack of interest on the part of the "manipulators" of American public opinion – politicians, media professionals, communication specifialists – in philosophy as such. In this industrial country, noteworthy for its advanced technocracy, decision-makers rely on scientific and technical experts, but they rarely think of appealing, on a social or political subject of general interest, to academic philosophers. Between the latter, on the one hand, and the politico-media class, on the other, the divorce is complete. Even more remarkably, both parties seem quite satisfied with this state of affairs.

To convince ourselves of this, we need only glance at the state of publishing, the press, radio and television in the United States.

Publishing is partitioned into two domains between which there is no communication. On the one hand, there are books for the general public, on the other, academic books. Among the first, mass-produced for entertainment or the popularization of technical and scientific knowledge, will be not be found any books of philosophy, or even essays exposing in an accessible style the major philosophical problems of our age. Among the second, on the contrary, can be found many philosophy books. But these are specialized books, aimed at an academic public, and bought almost exclusively for this public (i.e., essentially by the world-wide network of university libraries). Thus there is nothing comparable to the situation we find in many European countries, where it is not at all rare to see a philosopher (even a university philosopher) publish a book with a publisher who will try to reach not just an academic audience but the general public.

We see the same divorce in the press. There are in America many excellent publications specializing in philosophy, but the only people who read them and write for them are specialists. The mass-circulation press, on the other hand, whether daily or weekly, almost never devotes an article to philosophical books or issues. And even when the debates they echo might justify the intervention of a philosopher, none is invited to contribute. To be fair, we should cite a few exceptions. A bi-monthly like the *New York Review of Books* and a weekly like *The New Republic* regularly publish reviews of books of philosophy written by academics who try to be as comprehensible as possible. Two theoretical periodicals that appear less frequently, *Critical Inquiry* and *The Partisan Review*, even publish high-level articles on subjects relating to philosophy, sociology, history, and politics. But these publications are read only by a cultivated elite, that is, by a social class which hardly extends beyond the academic population.

Finally, there is little to be said about radio and television. Not because these media are, as some think, entirely devoted to entertainment: on the contrary, there are, particularly in the sector of public radio and television (NPR, PBS), excellent educational programmes. But, once again, the knowledge that these programmes aim to transmit to a vast audience concerns science, technology, and languages. It never, or almost never, deals with philosophy in the strict sense, or with debates of a philosophical nature.

Such a picture may seem excessively bleak. Is philosophy so completely absent from the social arena? Have the vast majority of Americans lost all interest for a form of thought which, at the end of the eighteenth century, was still so present in the minds of the fathers of independence?

Once again, we have to qualify this judgement: America is so huge and complex. Great intellectuals, in the historical sense, are perhaps rare. But they are not totally absent. Two major philosophers, in two centuries, have tried to play this role, and were rather successful at it. The first is Emerson (1803-1882), the second Dewey (1859-1952).

Both were prolific writers whose books, lectures, and articles dealt with a large variety of subjects, ranging from philosophy in the narrow sense to social issues of general interest. Both intervened frequently and actively in the debates of their times, and were concerned to address as large an audience as possible. Each of them could be considered, in his time, as the "moral conscience" of his country. Emerson is, as it were, one of the creators of the American dream in its noblest, most idealistic form. As for Dewey, his progressive convictions led him to fight, throughout his exceptionally long life, in favour of the extension of American democracy – and thus in favour of a democratisation of the educational system itself. Their audience was large, even if, today, they are not so often read, nor with the same respect, as are their near contemporaries in France, Hugo and Sartre.

It is true that, immediately following the Second World War, the United States was plunged into the psychosis of the cold war. Due to their role as the world's foremost economic and military power, international preoccupations, such as the confrontation with the USSR, the fight against communism, came to the fore, somewhat overshadowing internal debate on the functioning of American society. It was also at this moment that logical empiricism came to reign in American universities, pushing into the background philosophical tendencies that were too "committed" ethically or politically. Taken together, these different factors explain why, from 1950 to 1980, the divorce between philosophy and politics was so great.

This evolution, as harmful to one as to the other, began to be reversed about twenty years ago. With his *Theory of Justice* (1971), John Rawls was one of the first to show that a philosopher, and what is more, an analytic philosopher, could have important ideas to express on a problem concerning the very essence of social organization and the future of democracy in the world.

At the same time, a linguist who is also a prolific writer, Noam Chomsky, began to play, with his many stands on important issues, a non-negligeable role on the political-media scene, even if their deliberately provocative character, "third-world" and "anarchist", gained him many enemies. And even if the brief support he felt called upon to give, in about 1980, to the French who denied the existence of gas chambers has somewhat tarnished his image, at least in Europe.

The paths, very different, blazed by Rawls and Chomsky, have been courageously followed by other philosophers, in spite of the reserves their conduct has evoked in some of their colleagues; among these are Richard Rorty, Stanley Cavell, and Hilary Putnam.

This is, no doubt, just the beginning of a new direction. But it is a start sufficiently encouraging to prevent us from concluding that there do not exist today American intellectuals who are capable of being heard by their compatriots.

DEMOCRATIC PROCESSES AND THE TEACHING OF PHILOSOPHY IN AFRICA

Paulin J. Hountondji

After a description of the democratic changes that have taken place in Africa since 1989: their causes, current forms of political transition and the problems they raise, the author asks about the role of philosophy teaching at this time. Only the concluding paragraphs are given here.

If I had, in a word, to characterize the current philosophical situation, I would say first that it is marked, in Africa as elsewhere, by increased chances of speaking the same language, but also by the triumph of empiricism, the temptation to an absence of thought, which, in reality, leaves the field open to economic rationality of the most devastating sort, and, in another register, to all forms of integrism and irrationality.

Democratization has done away with one particular form of ideological oppression, that which, by fracturing human discourse, made communication impossible from the start. Not so long ago, one hesitated to speak of freedom in general, of justice, law, or democracy in general. The great dichotomies brought by the cold war forced one to specify whether one was talking about *bourgeois law* or *proletarian law*, *bourgeois* or *proletarian* freedom, justice, or democracy. Then, when it was least expected, first the Berlin wall, and next all the interior walls that partitioned language collapsed. Once again the possibility arose of unequivocal language, of using the same words with the same meanings, the possibility of communicating.

The Berlin wall was not only the material manifestation of a political frontier, it was also, on another level, generalized, institutionalized homonymy, unavoidable in any discourse about values. Its fall also meant the reconquest of meaning and the reinvention of language free of double-speak. Was it the *end of history*, as Fukuyama has written? Perhaps. Was it the triumph of liberal democracy and the collapse of alternatives? Certainly, although the simple recognition of this triumph does not necessarily authorize the philosophical thesis of the "end of history" (Fukuyama, 1992).

It is true, nevertheless, that the liberal model seems to stand alone today, with no credible counter-model opposed to it. This is no doubt an advantage, but it has its inconvenient side. It has the enormous advantage that we can once again speak to one another, but have we assessed the price to be paid?

The fact is that this reconquest of meaning was achieved by the elimination of one of the terms in opposition, hence by the reduction of an alternative that should, instead, have been resolved, by the evacuation of major problems that remain unsolved, of which we can be sure that they will come back in one form or another before long. The collapse of the communist block has been interpreted, perhaps a little too hastily, as the collapse of the communist idea, and the theory of inequality which was, in the history of thought, Marx's original and so far irreplaceable contribution, has been simply discarded, throwing out the baby with the bathwater.

In the domain of education, former ideologues have become silent, although all have not admitted defeat. They have just lost their jobs, after the disappearance of their party and the collapse of the system they represented. Silence has been imposed upon them, as they are well aware. The most opportunistic of them (for there are, of course, always opportunists) quickly turned their coats and stated to anyone willing to listen, that their support of the old order and its attempts to regiment thought had always been a cover, mere lip-service. The most courageous, however, those who had been sincerely persuaded by official discourse, have been rubbing their eyes as if just awakened from a dream, and trying to understand.

In the meantime, the Marxist-Leninist educational programmes have disappeared, sometimes not even waiting for an official act, a circular or ministerial decree, and there has been a return to the classical programmes of ideas and themes, comparable to those that existed in these countries before independence. More than ever, the project for harmonizing programmes firmly advocated by the Interafrican Council of Philosophy, in liaison, especially, with Senegal and the Cote d'Ivoire, has, in those countries where philosophy is taught on the secondary level, won over the national pedagogical departments.

It is obviously a good thing that such a dialogue has finally been re-established, and the last obstacles to the coordination of teaching in the region have been removed. But the negative side of the picture is a considerable reduction in "philosophical demand", the indifference of the public authorities towards a discipline that was once highly valued, and the "normalization" of philosophy.

As such, this is completely unsurprising. It is even appreciated by teachers and researchers, in that it protects them from State intervention and the State's desire for control. But there is a deeper problem. Beyond the fate of a particular discipline, what is really at stake is the attitude of the authorities towards thought in general, the place they give to reflective activity not only in the school but, even more importantly, in their own practice and in the determination of national policy.

What is in fact happening is that, with the process of democratization comes more than the triumph of freedom, the epi-
phany of an economic liberalism whose extension to the whole
planet has become a primary concern of the Bretton Woods
institutions. Forced to accept programmes of structural adjustment that were rendered inevitable, both by their own errors and
by the unfavourable international economic context, and wor-
ried about how to find the resources needed to finance these programmes, African governments most often see themselves as
having no choice but to accept, almost without discussion, the
famous "conditions" of the World Bank and the International
Monetary Fund. The truth is that they have gone to Canossa,
submitting themselves to the mercy of their "funders", abando-
ning all sovereignty, renouncing any attempt to define their
development projects by themselves, in coordination with their
people and independently of international finance. The most tal-
kative go even further and make of this abdication a government
policy, less by cynicism than by naivety, lazily invoking, when
they lack arguments to justify themselves to their public opinion, the diktats of the current masters of the world economy.

In such a context, by far the most pressing task is to call for a
more responsible attitude. Philosophy has here a new job: the
African philosopher should fight, less indeed as a philosopher
than as an intellectual, to re-establish the rights of theory and to
make all recognize that they have an obligation to think for
themselves.

In the final analysis, beyond the opposition between ideological jargon and short-sighted empiricism, and the pendulum
movement that swings from one to the other and back, the same
attitude persists, which should be denounced and combatted: the
tendency to let others think for us, to surrender intellectually,
which is the first, and probably the worst, form of irresponsibi-
lity.

In his struggle against facility, the African philosopher exercises, in his particular environment, the same function as any
other philosopher, that of fostering awareness, of waking people
up. If philosophy can contribute, in Africa or elsewhere, to the
promotion of democracy, it will not be by spreading or blindly
combatting specific doctrines, but by developing in each and
every individual, independently of doctrinal confrontations, a
sense of intellectual responsibility, a capacity to maintain a critical and open-minded relation to all ideologies, all philosophical and religious doctrines, an ability to think for oneself,
unmasking, behind the innocent facade of official discourse and
practice, the hidden sophisms, such as those which the logic of
world-wide capital has tended to impose silently, surreptitiously,
and to oppose to this alternative logics, and projects of society
that truly respect the rights of peoples.

III

THE INDIRECT POLICY

> *"Philosophy considered as a science, in the solitude of one's workroom or an Institute Academy is one thing, and philosophy as a subject for public instruction of youth in the name of the state is another. Do not lose sight of this distinction: it is the key to all problems".*
>
> Victor Cousin, 1844.

Overview

As we have noted, there are only two major possibilities: either philosophical thinking remains confined to a group of specialists, or else it is widely disseminated through education, and, perhaps, in appropriate forms through the media. The first possibility is rejected here. The second leads us to ask, among other things, when this education should take place, and what its content should be, in particular its political content.

Can the teaching of philosophy be limited to an introduction to the history of ideas, a panorama of doctrines, a series of summarized references? This would seem to be excluded. The unanimous opinion of professors of philosophy is that historical elements are useful, and often indispensable, but that the proper exercise of philosophical reflection cannot be reduced to such a collection of information.

But can this teaching transmit anything else than historical and cultural information? If we are convinced that it
is essentially linked with democracy, that it can help
consolidate and defend it, does this mean we give it the
explicit mission of transmitting democratic values?

According to this viewpoint, one would expect, for
example, the basic freedoms, human rights, tolerance, the
dialogue between cultures would occupy a central place in
philosophy courses. Their contribution to the education of
the citizen would consist in a kind of intelligent civic education. It would not concern the legal organization of elec-
tions or of popular representation, nor the separation of
powers. It would deal with principles and values. It would
shed light on the link between concrete historical situations
and the rules of reason. It would allow students to grasp the
very spirit of democracy and to understand its necessity.

This solution may appear coherent and positive.
However, it is not without risks, for it can lead to results
other than those aimed at. The teaching of philosophy
could lose its freedom to criticize. It runs the risk of being
confused with a form of catechism. In supplying answers
rather than asking questions, it may end up losing its
identity.

The major difficulty resides, once again, in the organization of freedom. As long as philosophy and its teaching
were private matters, this question did not arise in the
same way. But once the state takes over the training of
teachers and the development of programmes, it may be
tempted to transform philosophy courses into teaching of
official dogma.

This problem is at the heart of the relation between philosophy and democracy. It is easy to understand, not so
easy to solve. If we favour philosophical freedom and it
alone, the relation to democracy seems to disappear, and
the result is unacceptable: freedom destroys itself. If, on
the contrary, we favour political and moral education, the
dimension proper to philosophy is in danger of disappea-
ring, and the result is again unacceptable: freedom is destroyed with the pretext that it is guaranteed.

This dilemma is associated with the creation of state
teaching of philosophy. In the history of its establishment

in France, it can be detected before the middle of the
nineteenth century. Victor Cousin defended before the
Chamber of Peers, in 1844, the principle of compulsory
instruction in philosophy in the last year of secondary
education. He concluded by presenting this teaching as a
secular moral education. The goal was to standardize, not
to teach freedom. "In a secondary school, there are no
superfluous studies; everything is aimed at being useful,
practical. Here the risky and changing aspects of science
are ignored, in favour of its soundest and surest aspects,
and the teaching is based on these. The main goal is to
form minds that are healthy and vigourous and honest
souls", he stated during the debates.

To be sure, it was necessary to reassure the catholic
party, which feared the consequences of philosophical
instruction, and wanted its total elimination from the
secondary level. But, beyond this particular circum-
stance, such statements let us see how one of the first
examples of the democratization of philosophy – limited
to royal secondary schools attended by the children of the
bourgeoisie! – leads already to the problem of the "ins-
trumentalization" of philosophy, which we can see emerging today around the world.

The teaching of philosophy, which is often judged to be
far removed from contemporary realities, must not
attempt to become more accessible simply by taking its
subjects of reflection from current events. It would be dry
up and be emptied of its own essence by becoming a commentary on the news of the day. Of course, it should
accord a large place to the analysis of "political questions", in the broad sense – whether these concern the
theoretical foundations of power, of human rights, or of
international law. But it must not become for citizens a
course on "political education" in the narrow sense of the
term. The only thing that counts is its *indirect* political
influence. This is the third main finding that emerges from
the replies to the UNESCO survey. It is worth reading
them, to understand better the real meaning of the indirect
influence of the pratice of philosophy.

Data from the survey

The great majority of the replies emphasizes that philosophy teaching is judged too abstract. "It has remained
too bookish, too academic, too scholarly" according to
Professor Pierre-Paul Okah-Atenga (Cameroon). It is
generally criticized as being "too narrow, too dry, too spe-
cialist and not enough centered on the problems and sus-
pects that most interest today's society" notes Professor
Richard   Shusterman   (Temple   University,   USA).
According to the reply from Australia it is considered
"too narrowly, dry and analytical and abstract". "Current
programmes in secondary level teaching are generally not
appropriate" notes Professor Mauricio Langon, Inspector
for secondary school teaching in Uruguay.

Remarks like this come from all regions of the world.
In general, this teaching is judged to be not well adapted
to the problems of today. But just what is this lack of
adaptation? Does it concern teaching methods? The
topics discussed in the programmes? The vocabulary of
the authors? The textbooks and educational tools? These
questions are not sufficiently elucidated. The detailed
replies call for specific thinking and concertation in the
various countries, and above all in the various regions of
the world.

Among the policies proposed to improve this situation,
one idea would be to give preference to topics relating to
the important questions of our era. This is suggested by
the reply from Qatar: "We must move towards a new philosophy focused on current problems (especially atomic
weapons, genetic engineering, the new international or
world order, etc.) and on the ways to solve them". But we
can also ask if the true vocation of philosophy is to
respond to this type of demand dictated by circumstances.
As the reply from Morocco indicates, "the question is still
relevant of whether the teaching of philosophy should be
reduced to the 'direct handling' of current issues". No
doubt it is necessary, for there to be genuine philosophical thought, to maintain a certain distance. It would then
be appropriate to distinguish, concerning the "adaptation"
of philosophy teaching to the world today, different

registers: that of education, and that of the topics to be thought about. It is also necessary to analyze the conditions that make such adaptation possible, and the limits of its relevance.

For it is not obvious that adaptation is relevant. The idea that the teaching of philosophy should necessarily be adapted to the evolution of the world can be questioned. This is not a question of avoiding desirable improvements, but of emphasizing that we must also analyze this so-called evident idea. As the reply from France notes, the teaching of philosophy "is not perceived as owing its validity to its adaptability". A very similar remark occurs in the reply of Professor Christine Chevret (University of Nantes, France): "The primary vocation of philosophy is perhaps not to "adapt" itself.

Did Socrates want to "adapt" his interlocutors to the social realities around them? Or did he not try to adapt the realities to the ideals of justice and equality conceived in thought? His opponents were already blaming him for being a dreamer, for not being realistic. They knew exactly what they wanted, and wanted right away: power, money, pleasure. In a sense, this antagonism has not disappeared, and philosophers, throughout history, have never assumed the task of merely responding to the demands of their time.

It would obviously be simplistic to crudely oppose timeless reflection, unadapted and unadaptable, to historical development and its requirements. To avoid confusions and false debates, we should distinguish two main areas of meaning. This point directly concerns the theme of the education of citizens through philosophy.

In the first place, "adaptation" can involve the "use of new technologies": Plato on CD-Rom is no less philosophical than on parchment or paper. The same idea can be applied to the introduction of new topics for reflection: nuclear weapons or genetic engineering, for example. The question then is whether we can really speak of new problems, or if these technologies, while obviously innovative, just revive discussions about very old difficulties, long recognized and discussed. Should philosophy be taught only with chalk and blackboard, or pencil and paper? Must it forever take its examples from classical literature or ancient history, never speaking of Aids, today's fanaticism, political prisoners or the ethics of information? Adapting philosophy to such things amounts to giving it the means to be itself and make itself heard, while it continues to be its own particular self.

In the second place, "adaptation" can signify "obligatory submission to models, required conformity to norms", or "functional response to current demands". In this case, the honour of philosophy would be confused with what makes its very existence possible: its capacity to say "no". This form of updating would eliminate its raison d'être and its existence. Philosophy is indeed "non-up-to-date", that is, atemporal. Which does not at all prevent it from dealing with the questions of the day – on the contrary! But it does forbid it to sail with the wind and automatically align itself with the majority opinions.

Nor does this mean that the philosophical attitude consists in being systematically opposed to the general opinion. Refusing to share an opinion simply because it is widely shared is senseless. An idea is true or false independently of its diffusion or social status. The philosophical stance has nothing to do with conformisms, including that mechanical anticonformism which is afraid of any widely accepted ideas.

These first indications should be kept in mind in order to understand the replies to other questions asked by UNESCO, especially those relating to the role of philosophy in the training of citizens. Professor Peter Serracino Inglott, rector of the University of Malta, notes that a reply can only be an opinion and not a rigourously established fact: "To our knowledge, no scientific study has been made to determine the influence, apparently positive, of philosophy on the training of citizens." Although mainly subjective, these impressions are still not without interest.

On the whole, the possibilities are judged to be important, but the actual role of philosophy in this area is judged weak or non-existant. "The place of philosophy in the training of citizens is ridiculously small" states Professor Ngoa Mebada (Cameroon). "Philosophy does not play a

direct role in the moulding of citizens" states the reply
from Koweit. This role is judged "modest" in Portugal,
"minor" in Romania, "very restricted" in Lebanon, "very
indirect" in Australia. Professor Rada Ivekovic, who
taught comparative philosophy in Zagreb in ex-
Yugoslavia, notes that the role of the teaching of philosophy in the training of citizens is "important in the heads
of philosophers themselves, but in fact non-existant".

What is to be made of these remarks? They contrast
with the numerous preceding statements about the indis-
pensibality of philosophy teaching and its irreplacable
role in the development of the world in the future. No
doubt it is fitting to relate it to the relative absence, in the
philosophy programmes of most countries of the world,
of either political theory or democratic ideals as explicit
themes to be developed on their own.

It appears that reflection on tolerance, human rights, the
democratic tradition, or even on the foundations of international political relations is relatively absent in the teaching of philosophy. "The teaching of philosophy is not
concerned with these questions" notes the reply from
Cape Verde. These themes, emphasizes the reply from
Morocco, "are not at the centre of philosophy, as are the
foundations of law or the essence of man. Their place is
minor among the themes dealt with in philosophy teaching ." In the Russian Federation, according to the reply
of Professor Ruben Apressian, they occupy "very little if
any place".

Similarly, political philosophy proper has often only a
very restricted place. One of the replies from Pakistan,
from Zakariya University, states that "political theory is
not taught in philosophy. Only moral theories are taught".
The reply from Lebanon states that "this is avoided in
philosophy teaching ". The reply from Thailand indicates
that political theory is taught, adapted to the professions
concerned, to "administrators, judges, lawyers, religious
leaders and educators". Here we have specialized, almost
technical training, and not the education of all citizens.

It would be wrong to believe that this absence of explicitly political themes in philosophy teaching is necessarily due to censorship. It does not come from a decision

that is proper to some regimes and not to others. It does not appear to be due to a desire to systematically sidestep tricky questions. In fact, this absence is almost equally divided among countries, continents and cultures. There are, to be sure, states that prefer a summary approach to the question of human rights, freedom of expression, the free circulation of people, or of the rights of the non-religious and freedom to worship. For them, it would be better for these questions, and some others, not to be handled concretely and critically or in an insistant, detailed, or informative manner. This is not news. But, on the whole, the teaching of philosophy is no longer a place for open and persistent political confrontation.

The causes of this situation are not easy to analyze. The creation of new democracies after the collapse of dictatorial or totalitarian regimes is one factor. The general crisis of political thought and its lack of intellectual firmness is another element. The age of the great combats is over. In countries like Chile, where the reconquest of democracy provoked intense activity, some now diagnose a sort of "political apathy". Professor Marcos Garcia de la Huerta (University of Chile, Santiago) writes for example: "What is called the 'politics of consensus' has been and continues to be fundamental in the reconstitution and consolidation of the democratic system. But it also shows an obvious fear of dissent [...]. This fear of debate and of the confrontation of ideas seems to have replaced the terror which isolated the universities during the military regime. The closing and elimination of many academic units, both in Santiago and in the provinces, allowed the emprisonment and massive dismissal of professors, and the destruction of work groups in pratically all fields. The climate of mistrust and fear generated during this period has no doubt left traces. The situation accentuated a tendency towards scholastic thinking, and a flight towards themes allowing compromise. It transformed the past of philosophy into a refuge rather than a source of creation and inspiration."

This judgment, which would no doubt be valid, with nuances, for other Latin American countries, sounds like an echo of that of Professor Tanella Boni-Kone

(University of Abidjan), made at the International Study Days "Philosophy and democracy in the world" (February 15 and 16, 1995): "One might ask the question: where are the African philosophers? [...] Just when democratization processes have begun, the philosophy of professors is not yet reflecting on the immediate environment in which citizens and all those who, for one reason or another, are on the fringes of society live. Philosophy repeats texts at a time when it should be asking about the meaning of the daily lives of individuals."

This "retreat" of philosophy is no doubt just a transitory phenomenon, a temporary effect of the aftershock of recent socio-political mutations. Il may well be that, beneath this relative calm, in-depth work has begun, as yet invisible, but in fact affecting young people. In the case of Chile, the situation has been analyzed in its historical depth and complexity in a study of Maria Cecilia Sanchez, "Philosophy and democracy in Chile", specially prepared for UNESCO, to appear in another volume. Professors of philosophy always have a strong presence, in many countries, both in the national political conscience and in the construction of individual political consciousness.

There is not enough data to measure this. We can only note that, for the first time in history, the democratization of the teaching of philosophy is no longer, in certain cases, a slogan or a distant goal. It has begun to be a social reality. If we want to speak of "training for citizenship", this point is crucial. It can be estimated today that, in some countries, half of the new generation of students receives philosophical instruction. This is the case, for example, in Finland, where more than 50 % continue in school through the last years of the secondary level, where philosophy is a compulsory subject. In France also, with secondary level teaching, 50 % of the young receive some form of philosophical education. Other indications can be found in the table at the end of this volume.

Among the replies to the UNESCO survey, some people nonetheless stress the importance, qualitative and quantitative, of philosophy in education for citizenship.

This overall description covers very different realities, since the education can consist of marxist-leninist political courses or of reflections on the foundations of human rights and the pratice tolerance. Thus, according to one of the replies from Cuba, "most Cuban citizens have received a philosophical education. It is practically impossible to find a mid-level, specialized technicien who has not studied marxist philosophy". In Greece, in "National ethics" (provided since 1972 at the secondary level), tolerance, human rights, the democratic tradition and the foundations of international political life are treated as major among subjects, and in the more specialised philosophy teaching (provided since 1983 at the secondary level), such as in philosophy for high school students, they are also main subjects".

The attention paid to political and ethical questions seems on the rise, according to the indications received, in different regions of the world. Thus, the reply from the Netherlands observes that "nowadays sufficient tension is paid to social and political philosophy, philosophy of science and to ethics. Some thirty years ago too much attention was paid to history of philosophy". In Turkey, specific teaching concerning human rights and their philosophical foundation, which has already been introduced at the university level under the incentive of Professor Ioanna Kuçuradi, should be extended to the secondary level.

In Asia a network is being set up, at the initiative of the national commission for UNESCO of the Republic of Korea, for the exchange of thoughts, experiences and professors between a dozen countries. The goal is to develop philosophy programmes and specific tools adapted to the cultures and societies of this region of the world, and to organize better training for teachers. The establishment of networks of the same type in central Europe and Latin America, with the participation of UNESCO, is being studied. Each of these initiatives has the explicit aim of giving a new stimulus to thought on the role of philosophical education in the democratization process, and introducing new initiatives.

A first analysis

Let us try to summarize briefly the main points. Must we "politicize" the teaching of philosophy? The reply is "no". On the other hand, to hope for neutrality would be an illusion, and perhaps even worse. Philosophical education should not prepare students to live in a hypothetical world of ideas, but to live right here, in the world of men and women. This is a world of sound and fury, and also of injustice, oppression and subterfuge. Indifference towards the political is impossible. What then is to be done?

How are we to escape from this dilemma? Political education seems to be both impossible and necessary. To find a solution, we must take into account the basic distinction between the object of a discourse and its modalities: what you are talking about and how you talk about it. For example: it is one thing to discuss *on* tolerance, and another thing to discuss *with* tolerance. And speaking of equality is not the same thing as speaking in an egalitarian way. Or again: democracy as a subject of study and a lecture topic is distinct from a democracy of minds at work in a philosophy class.

What must be clearly distinguished, when we speak of the role of philosophy in the political education of citizens, is on the one hand the content of the teaching and on the other hand the way it is actually taught. Discussions on political questions should not be considered as the only effective type of teaching. In fact, we might even not deal at all with political subjects and still give "political" education for citizenship. Let us see how.

An exaggeration will help. Let's imagine an initiation to philosophy where the term "freedom of expression" is never even used. This fundamental right would not be mentioned among the concepts to be taught in the programme. No chapter of any textbook would deal with it, no course would discuss it. But in the philosophy class, the students will know that they could speak out and say exactly what they have on their minds. They will have observed that none of their remarks is ever censured or mocked. They will have acquired the habit, in their group, of criticizing what is said, but will have learned never to confuse rigour of argumentation with contempt for others.

These students will have a very precise idea of what freedom of expression is. They will of course have never heard the term. They will perhaps at first be unable to perform a conceptual analysis. But they will have effective knowledge of the concept of knowledge which cannot simply be reduced to a set of automatic routines. They will have experienced, in a conscious and constructed way, the rational requirement of their shared freedom.

The same point can be made with democracy. It is to be hoped that all issues related to the principles and values of democracy will be evoked in the philosophy course. But it would be unreasonable to ask every educational system to include philosophy teaching dealing in a detailed way with the problems of government of the people by the people, of the equality of citizens before the law, of the exercise of popular sovereignty, etc. But we can indeed expect of all not only that they should give philosophy an important place but that the teaching itself should constitute a genuine example of democracy. No doubt the teaching of philosophy is more appropriate than any other for real education in freedom within a framework of the rules necessary for any shared intellectual life.

This could be the true political meaning of the training this teaching can give. Not, to repeat, instruction in one doctrine or another, but the genuine discovery of the right of each to think, of an equal capacity to judge for oneself, and of the ultimate ignorance of all. This is, no doubt, an indirect kind of teaching. But it is still fully political. In this sense, philosophy teaching is a major school for democracy.

POLITICAL PHILOSOPHY AND CITIZENSHIP

Etienne Tassin

The study begins by jointly interpreting the crisis of political philosophy and modernity. It then analyzes the institutional division between "political sciences" and "political philosophy" and tries to define the proper object of political philosophy today. Before sketching proposals for a philosophy of citizenship, the author gives several indications for the development of political philosophy over the last fifty years. This extract only includes this section, the next to the last.

"Alienations" and the "Return of political philosophy Signposts (1945-1995)

It is possible to reconstruct (with all the arbitrariness such an entreprise presupposes) the path which, from the immediate post-war period to today, has led political philosophy from a realization of its impossibility to the signs of its reinvention going through the different stages which exhibit its alienation. Doubts about the consistency of political philosophy as a full-fledged discipline capable of offering a comprehensive view of democratic life, in the Western world just after the Second World War, took different forms, which can very schematically be divided into five stages, distinguished both chronologically and by the problems treated. As reductionist as this is, it allows us to see the movement of "alienation" and, also, no doubt more discretely, a movement of conversion or "return" of philosophy to political matters (and from these back to philosophy), which assumes the divorce described by Merleau-Ponty or Walzer, but without renouncing the philosophical elucidation of political action.

1) The first form occupies the immediate post war years up to the beginning of the sixties, most noteworthy for the development of the social and political sciences which substitute for philosophical reflection, invalid from the positivist point of view, a scientific apprehension of the social. It has been said that this development, the culmination of the affirmation of sociology begun in the middle of the nineteenth century, signified the end of the political. Whether it is methodological individualism, functionnalist or systemic analysis, the sociological approach to the social is characterized by two main features: 1/ a marked hostility towards political philosophy, correlated with a scientific claim to the positive explanation of institutions and social

behaviours; 2/ a radical misunderstanding of the political dimension of community existence, if not a real adversion towards the exercise of an active and conflictual citizenship. In a certain sense, and with the claim of the "ethical neutrality" of the social sciences and the rejection of any conceptual normativity, this approach to the social, by ignoring the political dimension, made impossible any theoretical elucidation of citizenship and its political implications. political science alienated itself from its object of study, political life proper, ignoring its meaning in order to account for its functioning.

2) The second form belongs to the theoretical heritage of Marx. It accompanied the "cold war" until the middle of the seventies. Whatever its variants and the interpretation given to it, marxist discourse and its ideological counterpart in political life displaced the centre of gravity of the analysis of political activity in two ways: first by deconstructing the political form of social organization and situating it at the socio-economic nexus of collective life (the relation of modes of economic production to productive forces); secondly by referring understanding of the social to an allegedly scientific theory of history. On the one hand, the political is dissolved into the social, of which it is at most a secondary emanation, on the other philosophy is denounced for its claim to make human behaviour intelligible, in favour of a supposed objectivization of the social (the economic base and the social relations following from it), made legitimate by a theory of history. In this way the heart of political action itself is emptied of its content, while the exercice of thought that was supposed to elucidate it is deprived of its elucidative virtues. The theoretical claim, transformed into ideology, wins out over political philosophy.

3) The third form of alienation of political philosophy is associated with the development of the social sciences, and is condensed in the formidable concentration of theories and disciplines united, throughout the sixties and seventies, under the label of structuralism. To tell the truth, political philosophy could not but succumb to the functionalist approaches dominant in the social sciences, identifiable not only in sociological explanation proper, but also in the attempts to produce a geneology of the concepts, behaviours and systems of social regulation of modern societies. An approach like that of Michel Foucault would invalidate the claim of political philosophy to elucidate the meaning of life-together, to reflect on what discriminates the just and the unjust, or to evaluate the different types of modern political regimes (in particular to distinguish between totalitarian systems and democratic regimes in terms of meaning) as much as would the descriptive analyses of a functionalist sociology. What such an approach gains in explanation of social functioning it loses in philosophical understanding of the political

conditions of human existence. In general, structuralism, like marxism, constituted an obstacle to the redefinition of a modern democratic political philosophy, all the more powerful because it claimed to cover the whole of human experience.

4) The fourth form comes from philosophy itself and marks it as the indelible trace left by Nietzsche and the Heideggerian interpretation of the historical destiny of metaphysics, in the form of the theme of "the end of philosophy". Philosophy can only be carried out as a meditation on the end of philosophy, thus it cannot have any practical interest in man's life-together. What is involved is not just that basic indifference (with rare exceptions) to the political which characterized the phenomenological movement in its attempt to recover the foundations of thought and the world of life, but an avowal of thought's basic incapacity to assume its temporal condition. The nietzschean-heideggerian heritage has continued to develop to the present, essentially in the form of a rhizomatic thought with the work of Gilles Deleuze and Felix Guattari, of the deconstructivism stemming from the interpretations of Jacques Derrida, or that of postmodernism associated with the analyses of Jean-François Lyotard. Against the background of what has seemed to some a "renunciation" a radical resumption of the project of modern emancipation which attempted by a "return" to – or a reactivation of – the rationalism of the enlightenment to refound in a pragmatics of communicative action the principles of a deliberative and democratic politics. The controversy about the question of modernism and postmodernism vigourously reintroduced the political question at the heart of philosophy and revived questions about the workings of political judgment and the status of community or life-together.

5) From still another direction came, in parallel to the debates concerning the status of reason itself and philosophical thought, the lines of questioning that emerged at the end of the eighties and the beginning of the nineties about the definition of the problems raised by a renascent political philosophy. In 1971, appeared John Rawls' book *A Theory of Justice,* which, from a liberal neo-Kantian perspective, reformulated the question of the social contract and the practice of distributive justice in modern liberal societies. If it is not an exaggeration to say that this book has defined the terms of the philosophical debate on the political question up to the present, this is also due to the fact that it was part of an intellectual context in which, to the conservative and socialist critiques of democratic liberalism there was added a republican critique forged in the rediscovery and reactivation of Florentine civic humanism, itself a descendant of the Aristotelian conception of the Polis and the Ciceronian conception of the *res publica*, and transmitted via James Harrington to Anglo-American thought of the seventeenth and eighteenth

centuries. For the critiques (and revisions) that this work inspired brought into focus the difficulties and issues which were to give a new vigour to political philosophy. Against the deontological paradigm of reasonable liberalism based on the priority of law over the good there arose either individualist critiques like that of Robert Nozick, for example, or communitarian critiques like those of Charles Taylor, Alasdair MacIntyre, Michael Sandel or Michael Walzer. Whether or not these were made in the name of a principle of the "common good" or the "good life" as opposed to individualistic atomism, in the name of "merit" of of a subject already embodied in a community and thus capable of "constitutive" commitments, in opposition to the disembodiment of the Rawlsian moral subject, etc., these controversies highlight the need to differentiate the orders of a common good and a public good, the registers of a moral determination of the reasonable character of choices and a political determination of public actions, of a private community centred on the values of individuals and a *res publica* formed to perpetuate life-together, in short to specify the properly political dimension of common existence, to revalue the sphere of the political and the ideas of virtue and civil liberty, to define the lineaments of genuine democratic citizenship. Three preoccupations come together here: 1/ conceiving a dimension of universalism of law compatible with the plurality of types of community existence; 2/ conceiving a dimension of civism compatible with the demand for freedom, 3/ conceiving a practice of philosophy compatible with the actual political issues of life in a community. The interrogation about justice, the forms of equality and civil liberty meets the question of a political implementation of the principle of universality confronted with the community or individual demands for the recognition of a specific identity. Thinking about citizenship has become a focal point for all the difficulties encountered in social, economic, cultural and political life. With justice, equality, liberty and universality, the question is raised of identity (private, social, ethnic, religious, cultural, political, etc.) and its problematic relation to the principle of citizenship, an interrogation fed by critical consideration of *affirmative action*, *political correctness*, multiculturalism, etc. A large number of studies are relevant here, centred around the work of Charles Taylor.

This last preoccupation requires that philosophy abandon the lofty position which is abstracted from real political communities and their problems, that it think about justice and citizenship from inside the cave itself, in order to interpret the meaning of the life-together which the philosopher shares with his fellow citizens. Interrogation about citizenship is, when taken seriously, also interrogation about philosophy itself as it attempts to see rationality in democratic society from the standpoint of the paradoxical indeterminacy which supports both philosophical discourse on politics and political discourse on rights and demands for recognition. If "thought about the political exceeds the framework of any doctrine or theory", as Lefort writes, this is because the political itself exceeds all limits, because it blurs the boundaries that men never stop trying to set up to live, and which they never stop contesting in the name of an increased demand for citizenship. By another route than that taken in the Anglo-saxon world, political philosophy in Europe has been led back to itself via a radical interrogation about "democratic invention", the institution of the social through conflict and the demand for the recognition of rights conceived as the generative principle of modern democracy.

The (re)discovery of the generative principles of the form of democratic society corresponded to a (re)discovery of political philosophy. In what sense is this a "return"? It is surely not a return of philosophy, which, supposedly, would have been badly treated in the various stages of its recent "alienation", nor is it a return of philosophy to some of its masters supposedly forgotten by history. As Jean-Luc Nancy puts it, to complain that we have lost real philosophy is simply to show that one has "forgotten what philosophy really is". The image of a return goes with the view of a crisis rejected as an accident, as if basically nothing of philosophy has really and definitively changed. Thus we should, as Miguel Abensour invites us, see in this philosophical interrogation of the political less a return *to* political philosophy than a return *of* political things themselves. The return to the neglected tradition is at most a restauration of the academic discipline, with all its capacity for speculative blindness to political things which the age has shown. The return of political things demonstrates the persistance of the political as a problematic locus for the emergence of the human and of meaning. The same uneasiness motivates the reflection of Jacques Rancière at the beginning of his last book, *Politics and philosophy*: "For some time now, political philosophy has been noisily affirming its return and its new vitality. Long shackled by marxism, which made of politics the expression or mask of social relations, and subjected to the incursions of the social and the social sciences, it has supposedly now recovered, with the collapse of state marxisms and the end of utopia, its purity of thought about the principles and forms of a politics which has itself been restored to its purity by the retreat of the social and its ambiguities. But this return raises problems." The return of political philosophy as a supposed branch of the philosophical tree seems to correlate with an absence of the political itself. This is because politics is not a just another objective domain of reflection for philosophy. On the contrary, "philosophy becomes 'political' when it entertains the puzzles or embarassment proper to politics", in short when it entertains misunderstandings without legislating.

IV

AUTOCENTRISM

*Between knowledge and ignorance,
there is love.*

Plato.

Overview

Does philosophy have a centre? Is it organized around
some fixed point? Does a single axis determine its perspective? We have no answer to such questions. However,
in a sense, the history of philosophies is part of this interrogation. Philosophies often believe they have found the
answer, but they also know that they have to keep look-
ing, for the centre is still missing, the fixed point invisible, the axis only tentative.

Of the many possible ways to classify philosophical
approaches, there is one which has perhaps not attracted
enough attention. This classification opposes those philosophies which seek the centre within themselves and
those which seek it in others. On the one hand we have
the diggers: the philosophers who seek roots, the native
soil of thought, the original sites. On the other we have
the nomads: the philosophers of voyage, of cosmopolita-
nism, of detours. On the one hand, we have philosophers
who want ever greater purity for philosophy, seek to detach
it from all that is not philosophy, want to make it more and
more autonomous, to make it stand on its own foundations.

On the other hand, we have philosophers who want to go
beyond, unlock gates, lose their identity, open their thinking in all directions.

This is, of course, a schematic, debatable, tentative distinction. But it is convenient and enlightening, since it
helps us realize that today we lack philosophers of the
second type. There are not enough border-crossers or
nomads. Our age needs minds that travel, that can play
the role of intermediary between different centres which
continue too often to ignore each other. The UNESCO
survey – this is our final overall observation – indicates
that there are still numerous barriers between cultures and
disciplines. Philosophy and its teaching, considered from
a world perspective, seem to lack openness, as if there
were a host of small self-centred groups existing beside
one another, with no communication or interaction between them. Thus one fundamental mission of philosophy
has still to be fulfilled at the world level: that of promoting reciprocal dialogue and discovery. Discovery not
only of knowledge but of traditions. Dialogue between
religious thinkers and between scientific schools.

This is a major task, and will take a long time, but the
means exist to carry it out: new tools of communication
already allow some to transmit texts and documents,
questions and answers, without delay, from one point of
the globe to another. In the near future, more and more
people will be exchanging information with each other.
Why should they not be able to reflect? Today, our problems are worldwide in scope, and our communication
networks are becoming global. Awareness of human solidarity, reaching beyond yet encompassing our irreducible
differences, is growing. But among the obstacles to be
overcome is the compartmentalization of the mind.

Our thinking is partitioned, our views fragmented. Even
when we try to look at broader horizons, the light we
bring is too weak. We continue to use as our frame of
reference our own habits and needs, whereas we need to
open our minds, expose them to the unexpected.
Philosophy can help us to do this, but for that it must not
fall into the trap of autocentrism, that is, of building
fences that enclose it.

This enclosure takes varied forms. First of all, philosophical education, according to the replies to the UNESCO questionnaire, is excessively centred on European thought and western culture. Rare are the countries where this teaching takes into account any books from other philosophical traditions. Almost everywhere in the world, the West dominates exclusively. This Eurocentrism must be overcome, and UNESCO has insisted on this point since its first endeavour. The conclusions of the international survey on the teaching of philosophy, prepared by Georges Canguilhem and published by UNESCO in 1953, show this.

They observed that it was "useful to develop, in education, comparative study of different philosophical traditions It is true that within each major tradition (western, Arab, etc.) the classic philosophers are generally studied without regard for national boundaries, but we should recognize the importance that a closer alliance would bring between the philosophical contributions of India, the Arab world, China and the West in teaching programmes that are too often limited to just one of these traditions. With such study of comparative philosophy students would be led to a more accurate and deeper appreciation of the importance of these diverse cultural realities, of their differences, their shared features, of the value of their conjunction". Nothing needs to be added to these lines, except the following: in this area, except for a few isolated initiatives, the situation has essentially not evolved.

Efforts have been made, as we will see, to introduce into teaching programmes the books and thoughts of various cultural traditions. But the real work of dialogue, comparison, common discussion, is still far in the future. Sometimes, in particular in some countries of Africa, there is a risk of falling into the opposite trap, rejecting Greek philosophical concepts viewed as foreign. If this attitude is followed to its conclusion, it could produce a symmetrical result to the situation it is denouncing and fighting: a single, self-centred view would simply be substituted for another. The terms would have changed, but the problem would be the same: our relationship to others would be ignored.

Data from the survey

"Philosophy students become familiar only with western philosophy and hear nothing of Islamic, Indian, or Chinese philosophy", observed Professor Michael Dummett of Oxford. The same state of affairs is noted in all the major European universities, and in the different secondary level systems. The self-centred West teaches only western philosophy. Programmes and textbooks are silent about the thought and philosophical texts of other cultures. The huge bodies of philosophy written in Arabic, Sanskrit, and Chinese are forgotten, or read only by a few specialists. In European countries, philosophy teaching, generally, does not deal with them.

Even the question of whether philosophy really exists in other parts of the world has been a topic of discussion for certain European philosophers! They claimed that the core of all rational truth and logical research was in the Greek miracle, and it was hardly legitimate to ask whether there was an Indian or Chinese philosophy. But that is not the worst of it. It was claimed by some, in this century, that philosophy could only be Greek. This was maintained, for example, for different reasons, by Husserl and Heidegger. Philosophy that was non-Greek, or non-European, for them, could simply not be found, its very existence was impossible: it would be a contradiction in terms.

This was taught, as a well-established truth, even as an undeniable historical fact. In the twentieth century, most philosophy textbooks in Europe repeated that the only philosophy was western. Asia, Africa, Latin America, the Arab countries may have had poets, mystics, dramatists, mathematicians, jurists, etc., but not philosophers. To give this name to their sages or thinkers would be an abuse of language. Such idiocies were very widespread. They reinforced the self-centredness of European philosophy, of which they were the product.

Why did this myth of the exclusively Greek origin of philosophy arise? The simplest kind of historical research would show that it is recent: it only really spread after the First World War. Why was it forgotten that in the nineteenth century, European philosophers looked towards the East, and in particular towards India? What is the significance, for the identity of Europe, and for the teaching of philosophy in general, of this still neglected past? This is not the appropriate place to examine these questions (in *L'oubli de l'Inde*,1989; I posited a kind of philosophical amnesia) but it was necessary to recall this overwhelming fact of philosophical Eurocentrism.

This particular form of autocentrism has had worldwide effects. The colonial domination of the European powers, and, more generally, the westernization of the world, have made strictly European philosophy an export. As the reply from Uruguay indicates: "No relation between philosophy teaching and cultural traditions is perceptible". This judgment is widely shared. Many correspondants, outside of Europe, have the same impression: philosophy, when its teaching is generalized, is often perceived as originating from somewhere else. Its universality is less apparent than its western particularities.

The problem is at its most visible in the former colonial countries which maintained or reestablished the teaching of philosophy after becoming independent. In rebuilding their own cultural identity, the area of philosophy poses specific problems, since they must integrate theoretical elements of their own culture into a subject matter from which is impossible to eliminate the elements deriving, for instance, from the Greeks.

In some cases, "the relations of philosophy teaching with cultural traditions are conflictual", as the Mali Ministry of Education observes. In other cases, the changes have begun: "Efforts have been made for philosophy teaching to integrate cultural traditions other than those for the West, mainly African cultural traditions", states Professor Ngoa Mebada (Cameroon). The dividing line between philosophy teaching and the intellectual heritage of African cultures has begun to be blurred. The two were unrelated", states one of the replies from Nigeria, "until recently that African philosophy is being introduced as a part of the curricula of most universities in Africa".

This issue is certainly one of the most important for the future, and also one of the most difficult to solve, since the assertion of cultural identity also takes the form, perhaps inevitably, of autocentrism. This was the case, for example, in Zaire. The report prepared under the direction of Professor Biangany Gomanu Tamp'no indicates that: "The philosophy of authenticity was one of the philosophical accomplishments of our national cultural life. It has marked all aspects of political and social life: the elimination of Christian names, food, dress, modes of thinking, criteria for political decisions, and politico-administrative organization. The philosophy of authenticity was the leitmotiv of the Republic of Zaire from 1971 to 1990. It has had much influence on the national cultural life of the people of Zaire".

The reply from Senegal states: "For a long time, the philosophy taught was of western inspiration, while Senegal is a mainly Muslim country (90 % of the population). Arabo-islamic philosophy had no place in the programmes. Since the curriculum reform, this tradition is better represented, although not dominant." This description in fact raises a double-barreled question: the relation between philosophy teaching and Islamic thought involves both the problem of the relation between the European and Arabic heritages, and the problem of the relation between rationality and faith.

Here again, there does not seem to exist an unique solution or a totally satisfactory outcome. In some Arabic countries the two kinds of instruction are more or less juxtaposed. In Koweit, for example, the main Arabic cultural traditions are studied in a course that deals exclusively with contemporary Arabic thought. Courses in Islamic philosophy treat certain cultural aspects of general interest. In other countries, tensions are perceptible, even if they do not lead to open conflict. Among the replies evoking a situation of this kind is the following: "Morocco is the land of Ibn Roch. This great philosopher is representative of a tradition which has integrated the debate on the relations between man, reason, and faith. But philosophy teaching is still viewed with suspicion by theologians, who tend to confine the field of philosophical reflection within the boundaries of their own axiomatic landmarks, and even to reduce philosophy to exegetic argument".

In general, the relation between religious beliefs and philosophical reflection figure among the themes frequently evoked in the replies received by UNESCO. But these do not all involve similar situations. In some cases, the domination of the religious authorities is clearly perceptible. In other cases, especially in many countries of ex-Socialist Europe, it is the philosophical institutions which have tended to return to Christian religious sources in reaction against the former domination of the official atheism of the communist regimes.

Very schematically, we can distinguish between the case of problematic, even conflictual relations with religions centred on their own revealed truth, and the relatively easy, even fruitful, relations in the case of the religions of Asia. In India, for example, we do not detect a global conflict between philosophical analysis and religious belief. In his communication for the study sessions on "Philosophy and democracy in the world" organized by UNESCO, Professor Satchidananda Murty stated: "Most of the elements of democratic faith can be found in the intuitions of the gymnosophists and sages of the Upanishads." The culture of India does not see a sharp division between philosophy, democracy, and religion. Professor Murty cites these words of Sarvepalli Radhakrishnan on democracy: "There is a continuity with the traditions transmitted to us down the centuries, with their stress on human dignity, the importance of the individual and the right to opposition."

Catherine Clément, a philosopher and novelist who teaches regularly in India, where she lived from 1987 to 1991, writes in her reply to UNESCO: "In a federation where the rule of democracy imposes a secular state, inevitably multicultural, the study of the philosophy of religions has particular importance: it is one of the foundations of Indian democracy."

A particularly clear expression of this Asiatic integration of philosophy, religion, and democracy is to be found in the remarks of Professor In-Suk Cha (of Seoul National University, and also director of the Korean national committee for UNESCO) made during UNESCO's "Philosophy and democracy in the world" study days. He states: "while most religions are quite different from one another, they are similar in that each attempts to resolve the problems of life and to give man the means of living in harmony with his fellows. Each one offers ethical and moral teaching which give human life meaning and dignity. In our part of the world, we tend not to draw a clear distinction between religion and philosophy. In fact, it would be appropriate to say that these two terms are interchangeable. All the systems of religious thought that predominate in Asia are centred on humanity. That is their common point, constituting that humanism which is itself at the heart of democracy".

Today, it is perhaps in the countries of Latin America that we find the most favourable conditions for a decentralization, or significant opening up, of philosophy teaching. As the study, published elsewhere, prepared by Patrice Vermeren for UNESCO on "The question of the philosopher and the citizen in the development of political regimes in Latin America" indicates, we can observe, in the contemporary history of the Latin America continent, a remarkable convergence of promising intellectual and political factors. We see both the search for a philosophical identity, distinct from that of Europe, and yet not hostile to it, and the desire for a renewal of democracy.

This renewal can involve the participation of philosophers, as the example of Professor Marilena Chaui (University of Sao Paulo) indicates. She describes the awakening of public opinion in Brazil after long years of dictatorship and terror. In her remarks at the sessions organized by UNESCO in association with this survey, she describes this process as follows: "Our philosophical association manifested itself in public by newspaper articles and interviews on radio and television. As our words reached the public, people began to realize that philosophy had a relation to society and to politics which none had ever imagined. Little by little, our presence became indispensable at political and cultural meetings, especially when the subject was democracy and rights. Our courses at the university were attended by all kinds of people, who had come in order to understand democracy through philosophy. We were solicited by the press,

radio and television. We created series of books on democracy and political philosophy which were sold out the
next day".

A first analysis

The question of autocentrism is not limited to educational policy or international cultural relations: it is a fundamental philosophical question. To begin with, we would
have, for example, to adopt Plato's distinction between
"the same" and "the other". We would then have to ask
why Plato states (and so many others after him!) that what
is similar attracts whereas what is different frightens. We
would also want to ask Plato for an account of the odd
parallel he makes between the philosopher and the dog:
"he growls when he sees someone he doesn't know,
although he has not be hurt by him, whereas he fawns on
someone he knows, even if he has not been well treated
by him" (*The Republic*, Book II).

Why Plato? Because this Greek reference occurs in all
the lists of classics, otherwise very different from one
another, received in answer to point 24 of the UNESCO
questionnaire. The makeup of such a list (roughly ten
names of philosophers considered to be classics) is
obviously artificial and somewhat arbitrary. But only in
part. The convergences and differences in the lists received (published at the end of this chapter) really do tell us
something about the status of the major philosophical
references around the world.

It is clear that international and intercultural reflection
is indispensable for an analysis of the obstacles remaining
in this area. They cannot quickly be overcome. But it will
not suffice merely to call for the exchange of ideas and
the circulation of people. If barriers, invisible but powerful, restrict philosophical education and block a true dialogue between cultures, we need to try to understand,
patiently and methodically, their construction in order to
propose concrete measures. The role of UNESCO can be
crucial in this domain.

This is not the only area in which UNESCO can contribute greatly to the broadening of philosophy teaching

around the world. The United Nations Educational, Scientific and Cultural Organization should not forget that the question of autocentrism also concerns the relation between philosophical and scientific instruction. The sciences, their methods, their capacities for conceptual invention, and their effort in theoretical elaboration, offer a huge area of exploration to philosophy. The close relation between science and philosophy goes back centuries, but today, it is too often cut off and considered to be a literary discipline. Because of this it is deprived of a very large domain of reflection.

The effects of this break are no less harmful for the sciences. Their teaching is frequently reduced to a set of formulas to be applied, more or less mechanically, rather than understood insightfully. Students accumulate theoretical and practical knowledge, but often do not know what scientific thought really is. They manipulate recipes without always grasping the principles guiding the scientific intelligence that produced them.

To conclude, our main point can be expressed in a few words: given that there is no specific subject proper to philosophy, philosophical reflection cannot remain centred on itself. If it does, it will die.

WHICH CLASSICS?

Point 24 of the UNESCO questionnaire says: "List at least ten philosophers who are considered as classics."

Some correspondents did not reply to this question. In the following list, some States are absent, while others may have several answers. The order in which the philosophers are mentioned has been respected.

AFRICA

Benin

• Socrates, Plato, Aristotle, St Augustine, Descartes, Pascal, Rousseau, Kant, Hegel, Comte, Marx, Sartre, Jaspers.

Cameroon

• Plato, Aristotle, Descartes, Hobbes, Locke, Leibniz, Spinoza, Hume, Kant, Fichte, Schelling, Hegel, Marx, Comte, Bergson, Sartre, Marcuse (Prof. Marcien Towa).

• Plato, Aristotle, St Thomas, Bacon, Descartes, Spinoza, Leibniz, Hume, Kant, Hegel, Heidegger, Sartre (Prof. Hubert Mono Ndjana).

• Plato, Aristotle, Descartes, Kant, Hegel, Epicurus, Marx, Spinoza, Rousseau, Hobbes (Prof. Pierre-Paul Okah-Atenga).

• Kant, Hegel, Husserl, Sartre, Bachelard, Bergson, Descartes, Spinoza, Aristotle, Plato, Hume, Leibniz (Ngoa Mebada).

Liberia

• Heraclitus, Parmenides, Socrates, Plato, Aristotle, Cicero, St Augustine, St Anselm of Canterbury, St Thomas Aquinas, Albertus Magnus, St Bonaventura, Duns Scotus, Leibniz, Kant, Descartes.

Malawi

• Thales of Miletus, Anaximander, Anaximenes, Pythagoras, Heraclitus, Democritus, Parmenides, Protagoras, Socrates, Plato, Aristotle, African sages, etc.

Mali

• Plato, Aristotle, Descartes, Spinoza, Rousseau, Kant, Comte, Hegel, Claude Bernard, Freud, Marx, Feuerbach, Engels (Prof. Yamoussa Kanta).

• Socrates, Plato, Aristotle, Descartes, Bacon, Berkeley, Hegel, Kant, Engels, Marx (Prof. Abdoul Kader Sanake).

Nigeria

• Plato, Aristotle, Kant, Locke, Hume, Berkeley, Descartes, John Stuart Mill, Heidegger, Hegel, Marx, Sartre, Spinoza, Leibniz, etc.

Senegal

• Plato, Aristotle, Descartes, Spinoza, Leibniz, Kant, Rousseau, Hegel, Marx, Machiavelli, Hume, Husserl, Heidegger.

Zaire

• Thales of Miletus, Heraclitus, Protagoras, Socrates, Plato, Plotinus, Aristotle, St Augustine, St Thomas Aquinas, Kant, Descartes, Hegel, Karl Marx, Heidegger, Wittgenstein, Sartre.

ARAB STATES

Jordan

• Aristotle, Plato, Al-Farabi, Averroës, Descartes, Hegel, Avicenna, Berkeley, Durkheim.

Koweit

• Plato, Aristotle, Hume, Descartes, Leibniz, Spinoza, Kant, Hegel, Russell, Wittgenstein.

Lebanon

• Plato, Aristotle, Pascal, Descartes, Levi-Strauss, Kant, Hegel...

Morocco

• Plato, Aristotle, Plotinus, Ibn Sina (Avicenna), Ibn Rushd (Averroës), Ibn Khaldun, Descartes, Spinoza, Leibniz, Kant, Hegel.

Mauritania

• Heraclites, Thales, Socrates, Plato, Aristotle, Descartes, Hegel, Kant, Ibn Rushd, Al-Ghazali, Sartre, Rousseau.

Qatar

• Plato, Aristotle, Farabi, Avicenna, Averroës, Al-Ghazali, Descartes, Hegel, Hume, Kant.

Tunisia

• Plato, Aristotle, Descartes, Spinoza, Ibn Rushd (Averroës), Kant, Hegel, Hume, Wittgenstein, Husserl, Heidegger.
• Plato, Aristotle, Farabi, Avicenna, Averroës, Descartes, Spinoza, Leibniz, Hume, Rousseau, Kant, Hegel, Marx, Nietzsche, Heidegger (Prof. Fathi Triki).

ASIA AND THE PACIFIC

Australia

• Plato, Aristotle, Descartes, Leibniz, Spinoza, Locke, Hume, Kant, Mill, Wittgenstein.

China

• Marx, Engels, Lenin, Confucius, Lao-tsu, Plato, Aristotle, Descartes, Locke, Kant, Hegel.

Russian Federation

• The parentheses correspond to the names of philosophers who would not be mentioned within the framework of philosophy teaching for non specialists. (Chinese philosophy schools), Socrates, Plato, Aristotle (Epicurus, the Stoics, Cicero), St. Augustine, (Origenes), St. Thomas Aquinas (Maimonides, Ibn Sina, Ibn al-Arabi, Al-Ghazali), Montaigne, (Valla, Giordano Bruno, Boehme), Bacon, Descartes, Hobbes, Locke, (Leibniz), Spinoza, Rousseau, Diderot, Voltaire, Helvetius, Kant, Hegel, (Fichte, Schelling, John Stuart Mill, Spencer), Marx, (Kierkegaard), Nietzsche, Schopenhauer, (Bergson, Windelband, Dilthey, Husserl), Solovyov, Berdiaev, (James), Freud, (Spengler, Moore), Wittgenstein, (Russell), Heidegger, (Jaspers), Sartre, Camus, (Mounier, Maritain and Jung, as well as Popper, Ricoeur and Habermas). (Prof. R.G . Apressian).

• Plato, Aristotle, St Augustine, St Thomas Aquinas, Nicholas of Cuza, Descartes, F. Bacon, Spinoza, Leibniz, Hobbes, Locke, Berkeley, Hume, Kant, Schelling, Hegel, Nietzsche, Marx, Husserl, Heidegger, Wittgenstein (Prof. A.L. Dobrokhotov).

Indonesia

• Pythagoras, Heraclitus, Parmenides, Anaxagoras, Democritus, Socrates, Plato, Aristotle, Zeno, Plotinus, St Augustine, St Thomas Aquinas.

Iran (Islamic Republic of)

• Descartes, Plato, Kant, Mulla Sadra, Ibn Arabi, Aristotle, Hegel.

Pakistan

• Socrates, Plato, Aristotle, Descartes, Spinoza, Locke, Hume, Berkeley, Kant, Hegel (Zakariya Univ.).

• Pythagoras, Heraclitus, Socrates, Plato, Descartes, Locke, Aristotle, Hume, Kant, Hegel (Univ. of Sindh).

Republic of Korea

• Western philosophers: Socrates, Plato, Aristotle, Hume, Descartes, Locke, Kant, Bentham, J. S. Mill, Hegel, Marx, Spinoza, Nietzsche, Heidegger, etc. Eastern philosophers: Kongzi (Confucius), Mengzi (Mencius), Lao-Zi (Lao-tsu), Zhuangzi, Mo-tzu, Hanfeizi, Chu Hsi, Wonhyo, Chong Dasan.

Thailand
• Buddha, Gandhi, Confucius. Plato, Aristotle, Socrates, Hegel, Thomas Jefferson, Huxley, Bacon.

EUROPE

Albania
• Aristotle, Plato, Descartes, Hume, Hobbes, Kant, Hegel, Fichte, Husserl, Sartre, Russell, Popper.

Belgium
• Plato, Aristotle, Seneca, Epictetus, St Augustine, St Anselm, St Thomas Aquinas, Descartes, Spinoza, Leibniz, Rousseau, Kant, Hegel, Schelling, Bergson, Husserl, Heidegger.

Bulgaria
• In secondary schools: Socrates, Plato, Aristotle, St Augustine, Bacon, Descartes, Pascal, Rousseau, Hegel, Marx, Nietzsche, Camus.
• In technical schools: Plato, St Augustine, Descartes, Rousseau, Hegel, Marx, Nietzsche.

Canada
• Plato, Aristotle, Locke, Berkeley, Hume, Descartes, Spinoza, Leibniz, Kant, Hegel, Kierkegaard.

Croatia
• Plato, Aristotle, St Augustine, Descartes, Spinoza, St Thomas Aquinas, Kant, Hegel, Hobbes, Hume, Locke, Wittgenstein, Nietzsche, Heidegger.

United States of America
• Plato, Aristotle, Descartes, Locke, Berkeley, Hume, Leibniz, Kant, Hegel, Wittgenstein. (Prof. Richard Shusterman).
• Plato, Aristotle, Descartes, Spinoza, Leibniz, Hume, Locke, Berkeley, Kant, Wittgenstein. (Prof. Richard Rorty).
• Plato, Aristotle, St. Thomas Aquinas, Descartes, Locke, Berkeley, Hume, Spinoza, Leibniz, Kant, Frege, Russell, Wittgenstein. (Tyler Burge).

Finland
• Plato, Aristotle, St Thomas Aquinas, Descartes, Rousseau, Hume, Kant, Hegel, Marx, Sartre, Wittgenstein.

France
• Plato, Aristotle, Stoics, Descartes, Leibniz, Spinoza, Hume, Kant, Rousseau, Nietzsche, Hegel, Bergson.

Italy

• Socrates, Plato, Aristotle, St Augustine, Descartes, Spinoza, Leibniz, Kant, Hegel, Bergson.

Luxembourg

• Plato, Aristotle, Saint Thomas Aquinas, Ockham, Descartes, Malebranche, Hobbes, Locke, Berkeley, Hume, Leibniz, Kant, Hegel.

Malta

• Socrates, Plato, Aristotle, Descartes, Locke, Kant, Hegel, Marx, Ricœur, Wittgenstein.

Norway

• Parmenides, Socrates, Plato, Aristotle, St Augustine, St Thomas Aquinas, Descartes, Spinoza, Leibniz, Hobbes, Locke, Berkeley, Hume, Kant, J.S. Mill, Hegel, Kierkegaard, Marx, Heidegger, Rawls, Quine.

Pays-Bas

• Plato, Aristotle, St Thomas Aquinas, Augustine, Nietzsche, Hegel, Descartes, Kant, Heidegger, Foucault, Hume, Locke, Popper, Marx.

Portugal

• Parmenides, Plato, Aristotle, Plotinus, St Augustine, St Anselm, St Thomas Aquinas, Descartes, Hobbes, Spinoza, Locke, Berkeley, Hume, Kant, Hegel, etc.
• Plato, Aristotle, Saint Augustine, St Thomas Aquinas, Leibniz, Kant, Hegel, Heidegger, Wittgenstein. (Faculty of Literature, Lisbon).

Romania

• Parmenides, Heraclitus, Socrates, Plato, Aristotle, Plotinus, St Augustine, St. Thomas Aquinas, Descartes, Leibniz, Hume, Fichte, Kant, Hegel, Bergson, Heidegger. (Prof. Corneliu Mircea).
• Plato, Aristotle, St Thomas Aquinas, Francis Bacon, Descartes, Leibniz, Pascal, Spinoza, Kant, Hegel, Lucian Blaga, Ernst Cassirer, Dilthey, Husserl, Bergson, Heidegger, Peirce and many more. (Prof. Petru Ioan).
• Kant, Plato, Heidegger, Hegel, Nietzsche, Husserl, Jung, Aristotle, Nicolai Hartmann. (Prof. Rodica Croitoru).

United Kingdom

• Plato, Aristotle, Descartes, Leibniz, Spinoza, Locke, Berkeley, Hume, Kant, Frege, Moore, Russell. (Prof. Michael Dummett).

San Marino

•Socrates, Plato, Aristotle, Plotinus, St Augustine, St Thomas Aquinas, Machiavelli, Descartes, Spinoza, Hobbes, Locke,

Montesquieu, Rousseau, Kant, Schelling, Hegel, Kierkegaard, Marx, Nietzsche, Freud, Comte, Croce, Heidegger, Popper.

Slovakia

• Plato, Aristotle, Saint Thomas Aquinas, St Augustine, Descartes, Locke, Kant, Hegel, Marx, Nietzsche, Husserl, Dewey, Wittgenstein, Heidegger.

Slovenia

• Plato, Aristotle, St Augustine, St Thomas Aquinas, Descartes, Pascal, Kant, Fichte, Hegel, Ales Usenicnik, France Veber, Udallaka, Aurobindo. (Prof. Janez Juhant).
• Plato, Aristotle, Descartes, Spinoza, Leibniz, Locke, Berkeley, Hume, Kant, Schelling, Fichte, Hegel. (Prof. Marjan Simenc).

Turkey

• Plato, Aristotle, St Thomas Aquinas, Al-Farabi, Ibn Rushd (Averroës), Descartes, Locke, Hume, Kant, Hegel.

LATIN AMERICA AND THE CARRIBEAN

Brazil

• Plato, Aristotle, St Augustine, St Thomas Aquinas, Duns Scotus, Descartes, Spinoza, Kant, Hegel, Marx, Nietzsche, Wittgenstein, Russell, Heidegger, Husserl, Sartre and Merleau-Ponty. (University of Brasilia).
• Kant, Hegel, Hobbes, Hume as classics (Federal University of Rio Grande do sul).

Chili

• Plato, Aristotle, St Augustine, St Thomas Aquinas, Descartes, Leibniz, Kant, Hegel, Nietzsche, Husserl, Heidegger, Bergson, Frege, Wittgenstein.

Colombia

• Plato, Aristotle, St Thomas Aquinas, Kant, Leibniz, Hegel, Hume, Marx, Husserl, Wittgenstein (Colegio Mayor of Nuestra Senora del Rosario).
• Plato, Aristotle, Descartes, Spinoza, Locke, Hume, Kant, Hegel, Husserl, Rousseau, Heidegger et Wittgenstein (Min. Ed. Nat.).
• Plato, Aristotle, Descartes, Kant, Hume, Locke, Spinoza, Nietzsche, Heidegger, Husserl. (Prof. Victor Florian).
• Plato, Aristotle, St Augustine, Descartes, Hume, Leibniz, Kant, Rousseau, Hegel, Marx, Nietzsche, Husserl, Heidegger, Sartre (Univ. del Cauca).
• Plato, Aristotle, Descartes, Spinoza, Leibniz, Kant, Rousseau, Hegel, Marx, Russell, Wittgenstein, Heidegger (Prof. Bernardo Correa Lopez).

Cuba

• Plato, Aristotle, Seneca, St. Thomas Aquinas, Bacon, Descartes, Kant, Hegel, Marx, Sartre. (Prof. Pablo Guadarrama Gonzalez).

• Plato, Aristotle, Descartes, Diderot, Kant, Hegel, Feuerbach, Marx, Engels, Lenin (Inst. sup. pedagogique "Enrique Jose Varona").

• Marx, Engels, Lenin, Hegel, Kant, Plato, Aristotle, Socrates, Thomas Aquinas, Democritus, Bacon, Locke, Hume, Rousseau, Heidegger, Nietzsche, Russell, Sartre (INVEST).

• Socrates, Plato, Aristotle, Descartes, Bacon, Locke, Hume, Kant, Hegel, Marx, Weber, Nietzsche, Husserl, Sartre. (CEA).

Nicaragua

• Parmenides, Heraclitus, Socrates, Plato, Aristotle, St Augustine, St Thomas Aquinas, Descartes, Kant, Hegel.

Dominican Republic

• Plato, Aristotle, Descartes, St Thomas Aquinas, Descartes, Kant, Engels, Marx, Nietzsche, Heidegger.

Uruguay

• Plato, Aristotle, St Thomas Aquinas, Descartes, Hume, Kant, Hegel, Russell, Wittgenstein, Husserl.

Venezuela

• Plato, Aristotle, Epicurus, Zeno, St Augustine, St Thomas Aquinas, Descartes, Locke, Hume, Leibniz, Kant, Hegel, Nietzsche, Husserl, Heidegger, Wittgenstein.

SCIENCE - PHILOSOPHY - TEACHING

Dominique Lecourt

All is not self-evident in the teaching of the sciences. I draw this conclusion from my experience as a university professor of philosophy who teaches only physicists. The feeling of uneasiness realated to me by my students, who, thanks to the Erasmus programme are both French and foreign, concerns not the forms or the recognized quality of the teaching they receive, but the content transmitted to them. It can be summed up as follows: "We are taught lots of equations, we learn to carry out procedures, we acquire certain skills. But we don't see the connections and relations in what we are allowed to learn." In other words, what they feel is missing in this educational programme is access to the *scientific thought* that was the foundation for and remains the support for the results they are supposed to master. They want to know what there is to Schrödinger besides an equation. It seems to me that this observation can be extended to all scientific disciplines and to all types of secondary and higher education. As far as I can tell, it is not contradicted any where in Europe. It leads us to a certain conception of science, and it is time that we recognized its philosophical roots.

These roots can be found without too much difficulty in the conception of science that was promulgated at the end of the last century, in a particular context. It was marked first of all by a transformation that affected the progress of basic knowledge, and by a questioning of the scientific ideal which had been inherited from two centuries of "Newtonianism". Another factor was the economic and social upheaval related to the so-called "industrial revolution", which profoundly modified the social status of science and scientists.

In physics, then considered to be the "queen of sciences", and the model for all others, the foundations of the mechanics on which all other research was based were showing unexpected cracks: the thermodynamics of Carnot and Clausius, with entropy, indicated that there were irreversible processes that did not fall under the reversible equations of classical mechanics. Electromagnetism was even more embarrassing. The best physicists of the day were divided among those who, like Helmholz, Hertz, and Boltzman, were trying to save the mechanistic paradigm, if necessary by introducing more flexibility, and those who, like Ernst Mach, were raising more and more fundamental doubts.

In spite of very violent, occasional conflicts, a common philosophical foundation was created that was supposed to deal with what has been called the "crisis of modern physics". It would in fact be better to speak of a strategic retreat, since the positions had been prepared in advance. These positions were those of *positivism*. Science, it was proclaimed, does not have the ambition of investigating the *causes* of the phenomena it studies, but only of establishing mathematically the *laws* which relate regularly observed *facts*. This thesis allows differing interpretations that are more or less radically empiricist, ranging from sensualism to conventionalism or pragmatism. The advantage to be drawn from this move is clear: if the subject of study is not the true nature of things, then the scandalous division of physics into two sectors governed by heterogeneous equations can be lived with quite comfortably. This thesis can be called "positivist" since it had first been formulated by Auguste Comte at the beginning of the *Course of positive philosophy* (1830), who had made it the cornerstone of a powerful philosophy of (the end of) history.

In all events the idea came to be accepted that the scientific approach could be summed up as a "method", consisting in the linking of observations by an adequate calculus. The use of the probability calculus seemed in fact to allow its field of application to be singularly expanded, so far even as to include the dream of a "social mathematics" envisioned by Condorcet.

We are now at the beginning of the century. The publication of *The Origin of Species* in 1859 had produced a new upheaval in another domain, that of "natural history", where for centuries people had been trying to reconcile Newtonian ambitions with the story of Genesis. In the same period Claude Bernard was founding "experimental physiology" and had introduced the key concept of the "internal environment" so that the organic could fall under physico-chemical law without it being necessary to deny the specificity of life.

Thus the positive thesis was working wonderfully well: it allowed reestablishment of the unity of physics and its history; and in a controversial domain that still smelt of sulphur and brimstone, it allowed reconciliation of some sort between scientific progress – observation of the *how* of phenomena – and the truths of religion, which provided the *why*.

It all comes together

But other elements were added, in a specific scientific context, which corresponded to the development of the "industrial revolution". The "driving force of fire" (S. Carnot) was now being rationally exploited in mines and transportation thanks to "machines appropriate for it development". The economic promises of electricity were turning out to be immense. The organization of production in factories was being replaced by that of large industry with its own division of labor. The working classes, increasing in number, were becoming the "dangerous classes".

The huge revolutionary explosion of 1848 had left its mark all over Europe. The best minds took up the task of working out a rational development of the new system of production that could guarantee social stability. References to science followed two distinct routes: one involved extrapolating a conception of society based on the most recent scientific progress. This was the case with Herbert Spencer, for example, who expected the thermodynamics of evolutionism to show that disorder always contains the seeds of a future order, one that is more coherent, better integrated and better adapted. The other path asked about the insertion of the sciences into the system of production. This is the path taken by Auguste Comte, inspired by the precedent of his master Saint Simon, who aimed on this basis to institute sociology as a science (and as a technique, since for him sociologists were supposed to become "sociocrats").

What does Comte say? That "all human work is either *speculation* or *action*". Either ... or. These are two distinct systems that should be cultivated independently. In the mode of speculation, we discover the laws of phenomena, which makes it possible to predict them. In the practical mode, appropriate to action, we seek advantages. Between these two systems, Comte seems to place an abyss, to set himself off from "those who conceive of the sciences only as the basis for the arts" (i.e., technology), because of the services they provide to industry.

But he nevertheless states that "the first system is the basis of the second" and that one should think of science as meant to furnish "the true basis for the action of man on nature". A concept allows him to maintain this (to say the least) acrobatic double stance: that of *application*.

If this concept has had the extraordinary success we know, that is no doubt because of its profound ambiguity, which allowed it to sidestep an embarrassing question present in its very formulation. In the *Encyclopedia*, d'Alembert had given it the following general definition: "Application of one science to another: this refers to the use which is made of the principles and truths belonging to the first to enhance and improve the second". The word "application" thus suggests first the idea that technical "procedures" are derived from scientific laws by deduction. But when, in its sixtieth lesson, the *Course of positive philosophy* in 1842 considers the question of "industrial mechanics" it states: "this mechanics is not at all, as is often believed, a simple derivation from rational mechanics". It is a "science of application". Engineers, of whom Comte to his credit sensed the decisive future role, will thus not be "scientists in the strict sense", but, states this graduate of the prestigious Ecole polytechnique, a separate corps whose "special role is to organize the relation of theory to practice; the "special theories" which constitute the contents of their "science of application" must be formed "*according to* the scientific theories proper", and this "according" (in French "d'après") has its own philosophical weight: it indicates a threefold relation of posteriority, imitation and subordination.

It seems to me that Comte, who was speaking to a Europe that he wished to save from revolutionary upheavals by uniting it around his theses, has been heeded all too well. The idea, in particular, that there exists a special technical thinking with an original inventive approach, has been effaced by the concept of application. What has been called "instrumental rationality" was conceived as simply the adjustment of means to ends, with no autonomy: the ends are set by production, the means adopted according to the previsions formulated in the basic sciences.

I said at the beginning of this chapter that "all is not self-evident". We now see in what sense this is so: we are following a path traced out in the middle of the nineteenth century. On the one hand, the sciences are taught as a compendium of results more or less quickly updated, and as a set of procedures of computation and observation that are unceasingly refined. On the other hand, technology is taught as a set of recipes "derived" from lofty theories that remain shrouded in mystery.

But it must also be observed that "it all comes together". As we have seen, these conceptions have been mutually adjusted to each other, more or less strictly, on the one hand with theses formulated in the sciences to respond "epistemologically" to a transformation of physics and to philosophically prepare the soil from which biology would emerge, on the other hand, with theses developed to evaluate a three-tiered social transformation combining the appearance of a new way of producing material goods, the emergence of new social classes, and the demand for a new political order.

It all comes together. Are we not seeing this even today? Is it not this "all", what is traditionally called a "world", which is unravelling before our eyes? If so, then there are conclusions to be drawn for our teaching.

The philosophical maturation of scientific concepts

No doubt the reign of positivism has not yet allowed us to learn all we can from the great upheavals that affected the physical sciences in the early decades of the present century. But still the theory of relativity and quantum mechanics, to take only the two major theories we have at our disposal, teach us a quite radical lesson. We know that the truly fecund scientific ideas do not emerge from simple observation of the "facts", but rather from "speculations" which go far beyond observation, and that a concept must include in its definition the experimental conditions of its realization. We have also learned that a theory cannot be reduced to mere computation: it can only be constituted at the price of an uninterrupted and painful struggle with observations, perceptual or intellectual, to which we "spontaneously adhere" because we have received them from the set of institutions in which we are destined to live. But scientific thought, by its essence, is precisely not a thought that adheres, or adhesive thought, it is rather thought which "doubles itself" (Bachelard), a thought which never ceases judging itself so that it can make progress through successive revisions.

But on what does its judgement of itself rest, in these decisive moments, if not the presuppositions it has inherited from a past to which it is not the only contributing element, since other forms of human thought and practice are also involved? Consider Newton's notion of absolute space, and the set of positions it could muster, from afar, in psychology, morals, politics, and even theology. These explain without the slightest doubt why it was so hard to get rid of it, even though Newton himself had been so cautious when he proposed it.

This is what should motivate us to reintroduce *the philosophical maturation of scientific concepts into our science teaching*. For then science will open itself to what is outside it. Instead of imposing its authority as an object of belief, it will be able to train the minds of its students to see the adhesive forms of their thinking as they really are. In French we have an expression that designates nicely the attitude this kind of teaching can produce, it is "disponibilité d'esprit", literally "availability of mind".

Once again, it all comes together. The teaching of technical disciplines can now, from the same perspective, rethink its intellectual and social status. The verbal unction of the "logos" is not enough to accord to technique, which has become "technology", recognition of the dignity it can rightfully claim. Not as a lesser species of science teaching, but as the teaching of a specific type of thought and rational activity. It will then be possible to show that technique creates its own values, of which innovation, a consciously assumed break with the past, is the most characteristic; that these *values* are carried by norms which always constitute a system; that, however, the action of these norms is always motivating, inspirational, and that the system is open, always open to the future, constantly anticipating new forms of use. In short, *technical thinking*, as such, can help us to know what *anticipate* really means, instead of continuing to believe that the future is nothing more than a prolongation of the present!

What can be done

"...what is rationally founded and valid for theory is also valid for practice."
Emmanuel Kant, 1792.

THE TEACHERS, THE BOOKS AND THE SCREEN

> *"He who takes a mirage for water, and once
> he gets to it, convinces himself that there is no
> water, he is truly mad."*
>
> Ratnâvalî (*The wreath of jewels*)

Overview

UNESCO was founded for action. Its goal is not pure
knowledge. If it collects data, it is to make it available to
Members States or non-governmental organizations, to
provide useful information for their programmes of
action. UNESCO also has the mission of reviewing the
initiatives proposed by its Members States. The present
survey could thus not be content with merely collecting
information. It was also very important to collect pratical
proposals and submit them to its readers.

What can be done to develop philosophical education?
What goals should have priority? What choices should be
made for international action? By what means can philosophical education be developed outside of formal study?
Some preliminary suggestions in answer to these questions will be found in this chapter. They are organized
around two viewpoints that are not mutually exclusive,
but can be considered as complementary.

The first of these considers philosophy from the scholarly and academic point of view. From this perspective,

acting for the development of philosophical education involves increasing its presence in different courses of study, rounding out the student curriculum, worrying about teacher training, rethinking pedagogy, reformulating programmes, updating textbooks, stocking libraries, promoting translation and publishing strategies, supporting international research through a system of fellowships and exchange programmes, etc. All these things are important, even vital. Some are exclusively a matter of national decision, others necessarily fall into the framework of international cooperation and require active support from the philosophical community. What they all have in common is that they treat philosophical reflection only as a scholarly discipline.

Philosophy extends far beyond this setting. It partakes of it, but cannot be reduced to it. The second point of view stresses this "virtual omnipresence" of philosophical analysis and critique. It includes the following: relating concepts to current events, showing how a philosophical perspective helps us see the same events in a different way, emphasizing the political implications of the freedom to doubt, inviting contributions from philosophers to reflect on world problems, thinking about the use of all currently available technologies to create new forms of initiation to philosophy via radio, video, computers, multimedia, etc. The major preoccupation here is no longer the school and university public, but "the public" itself.

This is no doubt where world-wide action could turn out to be particularly relevant, for while numberless local initiatives depend on the social and cultural habits specific to a given country, the implementation of broad-scale programmes of this sort can only result from international collaboration. It is indispensable both for the elaboration of projects and their realization. The contributions of philosophers from different cultures to the analysis of the questions asked by mankind today can only be handled by an intergovernmental organization like UNESCO. It is also part of its mission to stimulate international reflection on the specific difficulties arising from the relations between philosophical modes of thought and computer technologies.

These two viewpoints are undoubtedly different. They do not involve the same conception of the relation between philosophy and democracy. Furthermore, they give rise to quite distinct programmes of action, according to the aspect one chooses to highlight. But there is no obligation to choose one to the detriment of the other, for the approaches are neither contradictory nor incompatible. Not only can they coexist, but the programmes they inspire can mutually reinforce each other. The more philosophy teaching is a part of education, the more the presence of philosophy in the other sectors of cultural life is facilitated.

We must stop crudely opposing the old and the new, the book and the screen, the word and the image, pure thought and impure action. What the main developments of this century evoke, on the contrary, is that these oppositions, instead of hardening into irreducible antagonisms, have given rise to unforseen links and inventive synergies. Recordings have not eliminated concerts, television has not killed cinemas, the net will not mean the end of printed books. Things will change, given the profound mutations taking place. But there is no reason to despair for the life of the mind. That is what is indicated by the responses to the UNESCO questionnaire, in the very diversity of the concrete measures suggested.

Data from the survey

For many correspondants, from very different regions, the first measure taken should be to extend the teaching of philosophy. This does not mean merely artificially adding a few more course hours at all levels and in all sectors. Most of the time, the "generalization" of philosophy teaching is advocated for levels of study where it already exists. Thus, in higher education, there are proposals to create philosophy departments in universities that lack them. The setting up of philosophy programmes, optional or compulsory, in scientific and technical courses is also suggested. For example, in Pakistan, Professor Bahauddin (Zakariya University) suggests the "creation in all universities of a department of philosophy for students

on campus who already have a degree". In the Republic
of Korea the national committee for UNESCO would like
to see the development of "the teaching of philosophy,
optional or compulsory, in secondary and higher education". In Belarus, Professor V. K. Lukashevitch judges
that "all the students working for higher education diplomas should be required to take an examination in philosophy". Other countries, where philosophy is present at
the secondary level, suggest that this training be extended
to the technical sections, or to the last years of secondary
school, or, as an option, to the first years.

Some responses encourage the experimental teaching
of philosophy to children. There are already many such
experiments in the world and it would be interesting to
study them one day. But for the time being, there are more
urgent things to do. Human and material means are so
lacking that this must be our priority.

The two needs most strongly emphasized in this area
concern the training of teachers and the providing of educational tools, above all textbooks and set texts. What is
unanimously called for is better training of teachers, more
opportunities for them to obtain study grants, and advanced or refresher courses to help them update or improve
their knowledge. This requirement can be heard from
almost all regions. It is particularly strong in Africa,
where most of the responses insist on this point, but also
in the Russian Federation and Belarus, where the teaching
of philosophy, to judge by the responses UNESCO has
received, is in a state of crisis.

The question of teacher training is not particular to philosophy. The need to pay teachers an adequate salary, the
possibility of continued training, and a sufficient supply
of indispensable educational tools, are not specific to philosophy. It is obvious that these requirements apply to all
other disciplines, although there are no doubt differences
of priority and emphasis in the case of philosophy.

As is well-known, the teacher's personality is a more
important factor than it is in other fields. There are several reasons for this: the greater freedom usually granted to
philosophy teachers in the way they organize the syllabus
subjects, the novelty of the philosophical approach for the

pupils, the emotional involvement caused by most of the subjects treated. All the more reason to require that philosophy teachers be given excellent training and the possibility to improve continuously through international exchanges and sufficient information.

So, the first demand is for teachers, as well as for books, since the two go together. What is expected of the philosophy teacher is not the teachings of a sage or a prophet, but the help of an experienced reader given to inexperienced ones. Without texts, without direct and easy access to the works themselves, teachers are helpless, and students are deprived. That is why, from Europe to Asia and from Latin America to Africa and the Arab States, books are always awaited, hoped for, irreplaceable. We need to "publish more philosophical works in low-price paperback form", writes Professor Szabo of Hungary; we should favour "the production and distribution of philosophy textbooks that are more accessible to students, and publish correctly translated and annotated editions of the philosophical classics" states the response from the Republic of Korea. And Professor T. M. Tusoma of Belarus says that it is indispensable to have "publication of the philosophical classics in inexpensive editions".

We need to "favour the creation of modern libraries adequately supplied with philosophical works, and envisage measures that will allow the acquisition of philosophical works at acceptable prices", suggests Professor Simon Menye Ngono of Cameroon. One of the responses from Nigeria stresses that it is desirable to "have a greater number of works of philosophy in libraries". It ought to be possible to "supply educational institutions with philosophical works by creating specialized libraries", states the response from Senegal, which also notes that it is "indispensable, since the 1970's programme reform, to place works (textbooks and anthologies) at the disposition of students, which is not yet the case". It is necessary to "increase the number of textbooks translated", states the response from the Islamic Republic of Iran. We must "increase the number of books dedicated to the teaching of philosophy at the secondary level", emphasizes the response from the Syrian Arabic Republic.

The need for philosophy books is stated everywhere. It
is clearly urgent to develop major international projects in
this domain. There are many possibilities. One of them
was raised within UNESCO in 1946 and 1953, also in
1980, and it is still relevant. The idea would be to prepare,
with the help of a committee of experts, a series of
volumes collecting representative works from the major
philosophical traditions. These anthologies could then be
translated into different languages and furnished to educational institutions in a large number of countries. One
can also imagine, as a simple and relatively inexpensive
project, the creation of a centre of information on philosophy books donated by individuals or institutions. As
suggested by Professor Donald Davidson (University of
Berkeley, USA) at the international meeting "Philosophy
and democracy in the world" organized by UNESCO on
February 15th and 16th, 1995, this centre would collect
all offers and give information on availability.

Still in the area of education, we received suggestions
concerning changes that could be made to the traditional
approach, sometimes considered too "traditionalist", to
the teaching of philosophy. Thus the response of
Professor Peter Serracino Inglott, rector of the University
of Malta, suggests "encouraging philosophy students to
offer their personal ideas in their educational establishments and in public. The general public could thus be
made more aware of the importance of philosophy." In
Bulgaria, Prof. Tzotcho Boyadjiev (Saint Clement of
Ohrid University, Sofia) has taken an original initiative:
"philosophers should make the teaching of philosophy in
different countries commensurable. We have taken a step
in this direction by organizing an international Olympics
in philosophy for secondary students. In Bulgaria six
national Olympics have already been held. During the last
two, we had guests from other countries (Germany,
Hungary, Poland and Turkey), and we intend to pursue
and extend this initiative".

Instead of national decisions and limited cooperative
actions, some propose a sort of world "platform" which
would set out a general framework for philosophy teaching. In this spirit Professor A. L. Dobrokhotov

(Moscow University, Russian Federation) writes: "We need an international programme that could establish a set of practical recommendations for the teaching of philosophy to different age groups and at different levels, avoiding a levelling to the lowest common denominator and standardization, and taking into account as much as possible the plurality of cultural traditions, as well as the current world crisis". No doubt a comparable inspiration motivates the response from Nicaragua: "to create 'Centres for the Study of Philosophy' in order to resolve, at least on the theoretical level, the problems of humanity. To form at the world level, with the help of our century's thinkers, a 'democratic philosophy'."

Nevertheless, what philosophy teachers all over the world are asking for, rather than educational guidelines, are chances to meet one another, to learn about common problems. In fact, the community of philosophers want, through a discussion of their differences, to become a real community. Thus the response from the University of Malta proposes "frequent holding of regional and international conferences for all those involved in the teaching of philosophy". The response from Cape Verde also insists on the need to encourage "contacts with institutions and people from other regions involved in the field of philosophy". Many responses insist on the fact that, in philosophy, brief encounters are not enough. We must also envisage the possibilities of longer-lasting contact. Only then can the context for true dialogue be created. Conferences can reduce the isolation of some researchers, but too often they only produce a juxtaposition of positions rather than dialogue.

It should not be forgotten that the real meeting of minds takes time. We will achieve little in the way of dialogue between the world's philosophies if we ignore this essential factor. For scientists, a system of common references is immediately available. A philosopher must discover everything about what the other is thinking: behind identical terminology may be lurking different concepts, sometimes radically different. By what miracle could this difficult reciprocal learning process be accomplished in just a few hours, or even a few days? Philosophical thought has its own slow rhythms. It is not by chance that already in 1946 the question of a "Philosophers' House" had been raised at UNESCO. The project was never realized, but it is still quite relevant.

The relation between philosophy and the present world is the guiding idea of the second set of practical proposals to be found in the responses. There is a convergence of many themes here: relations between philosophers and the general public, the role of concepts in the age of media we have now entered, the use of new electronic means to renew the teaching of philosophy. Two main points can be distinguished: first, an actualization of the themes of philosophical reflection, and second the "popularization of philosophy" through new modes of communication. It would be simplistic to take these two issues to be essentially identical, or to think that they are necessarily linked. We can perfectly well imagine a renewal of thinking, focussing on the most pressing problems of the modern world, but addressed exclusively to an elite, or diffused only by traditional means. We can also conceive of a type of teaching that is wholly conventional in its theoretical content but which is diffused by electronic servers, CD-ROM, and videocassettes. Obviously one must not confuse innovative techniques and innovative ideas.

But it is nevertheless legitimate to consider these two issues together. If we are to address the general public, through video and, soon, through all sorts of electronic media, it is reasonable to think that the analysis of relevant global issues will be of primary interest, whereas remote and ancient metaphysical disputes are likely to quickly become tiresome. "Making philosophy accessible to a larger public" means both "choosing themes of reflection that are relevant to contemporary life", and "using techniques of diffusion that can reach the greatest possible number". The two interpretations can be intended separately or simultaneously.

What exactly is meant by the renewal of the themes of philosophical reflection? Italy's response helps us understand this better: "The new programmes deal with current issues such as ethics in technology, the environment, the future, and solidarity. With respect to methodology, we encourage young people to study the texts of philosophers using more rigourous linguistic and logical analysis. At present, it is important that the teaching of philosophy be accessible to all young people, that it deal with topics of current interest, that it be an instrument for the expression of points of view, and that it foster the resolution of conflicts by argument instead of by violence. The more philosophical reflection is concerned with the questions that worry and mobilize people today, the more it will be attended to. This point is made in the response from Qatar: "Philosophy will only flourish if it deals with the problems facing the world community today, that is the real problems threatening the survival of mankind, such as atomic weapons, environmental degradation, war, genetic engineering and issues of tolerance, freedom, democracy and human rights, in addition to the problem of the goals of science and the uses of technology, and their limits." Very similar remarks appear in responses coming from all regions of the globe. Thus Professor Suzana Villavicencio (University of Buenos Aires, Argentina) suggests that thinking should focus on "the major ethico-political themes of the day, the philosophy of technology, issues in ecology, citizenship, and rights, the history of ideas in relation to political processes, and, in general, greater integration with current problems".

The use of television and videocassettes is often raised. However it is less frequently mentioned than the need for inexpensive books. This is understandable for many reasons. First of all, there are the difficulties, both educational and financial, connected with the newer media. Their manufacturing cost is much greater than that of books, and their use more limited, depending on the availability of a VCR, television set, electricity, etc. The simplicity and variety of books contrasts with the technical and economic constraints of the audio-visual media.

The same considerations apply, even more strongly, to multimedia productions. Obviously philosophical initiatives should be encouraged in this new area. We should support all creation that allows philosophical reflection to take a concrete form in unaccustomed environments.

Suggestions of this kind occur frequently in our responses. For instance Kuweit suggests "recourse to multimedia in the teaching of philosophy", and we find the same idea in the responses of Pakistan and other countries. This is surely an idea with a future.

A first analysis

Perhaps the issue of multimedia is still way ahead of today's reality. While it is true that computers equipped with CD-ROM drives are more and more common around the world, the proliferation of such devices has hardly begun to reach the general public even in the richest countries. It seems difficult to state, at least in the final years of the current century, that the most educational of the electronic devices can as yet be considered a hallmark of "philosophical education for all". We must not forget that, for the present, in many countries around the world, computer equipment is still quite rudimentary, or else reserved for an elite. The cost of computers, their relative fragility, their complexity, do not authorize us as yet to consider them to be truly popular cultural tools. Inexpensive books, widely distributed, are today the more practical and effective instruments. And this will probably continue to be the case for a long time.

This does not at all mean that the computer is unimportant, or has no role to play. But its main function, in the immediate future, from the viewpoint relevant here, is as an instrument of communication. The fact that these once closed boxes can now be connected to worldwide networks allows the instantaneous and inexpensive exchange of information. Access is now possible, via Internet and other networks, to entire libraries, electronic publications, discussion forums, and data bases of all sorts. Until the day, probably far off, when truly "everyone" will have access to these networks, at least the collective use of them can be facilitated.

A minimum amount of equipment, a computer, a modem, a printer, will allow users not only to consult library catalogues, but to download entire books. In a few minutes, a centre of documentation, a philosophical society, or a group of students can print a text which is physically located thousands of miles away. They will then be able, if this text is in the public domain, to reproduce and circulate it. While this cannot replace books, and does not solve the problem of the translation of philosophical classics, it is a powerful remedy for isolation. That is why the international community should provide specific assistance to connect the least favoured nations.

There is also a risk, once one is connected to the networks, of having to deal with too much information. Perhaps in the near future, a new type of vertigo will be diagnozed! But common sense leads one to think that this is less harmful than deprivation, and easier to solve. Common sense also tells us that the different cultural ways and communication means at our disposal are not necessarily opposed. The teachers, the books and the screen can and must create synergies.

INTERNET AND HUMANISM

Luca M. Scarantino

The study first analyzes the contribution of computer techno-logy to philosophical research, then the possible educational uses of the CD-ROM in philosophy; and lastly, the role of inter-national networks in the exchange of information. Only the final pages of this study are given here.

The arrival of the age of global communication *via* electronic networks is changing everyday life more than any other media in recent history. The very speed with which we can communi-cate with anyone on the planet is producing an unprecedented transformation of our daily lives. Unlike those electronic tech-niques (CD-ROM and hypertext), which function more as spe-cialized professional tools explicitly conceived for educational use, Internet directly affects the way we communicate with the outside world, and does so more powerfully than any other know technique.

As perhaps not all are aware, the first networks (Arpanet, for example) were developed to fill a basic hardware need, and have progressively developed to their current dimensions. This helps us understand what distinguishes them from other educational hardware: the potentialities of Internet are relevant to the inter-national spread of philosophical culture, and not to didactic methodology. We are dealing here with a completely different level.

Consider, for example, the case of Jim O'Donnell, a professor at the University of Pennsylvania, whose doctoral course on the philosophy of St. Augustine was transmitted on Internet, which not only gave students access to it but also turned the course into a sort of continuous discussion on the prescribed text. Even though this does not at first seem very different from traditional methods of distance teaching, the fundamental novelty of this relationship lies in the possibility for unlimited exchange of information in real time, and for broadcasting it all over the world. What we have here is a capacity for constant interactive exchange.

Internet has thus become a powerful instrument of world-wide teaching with a potential for eliminating national bounda-ries. More than any specific educational technique, the ongoing development of electronic connectivity holds the promise (I am thinking especially of the younger generations in the less deve-loped countries) of a progressive reduction of cultural exclu-sion.

However, we cannot be absolutely sure that the almost total freedom of Internet use today will last into the future. One of the main problems of Internet communication, affecting everything from data bases to mailing lists, is the ever-increasing amount of work for those in charge of the electronic structures. This makes it conceivable that the services handled by Internet will progressively be transformed into services managed by universities (in the case of philosophy) and other research institutions, who will then have to provide specifically trained and remunerated personnel. Moreover, the online services offered are bound to develop and improve. Internet will not be able to avoid professionalization, although it is perhaps premature to speak of this.

It is clear, then, that in the area of international cooperation Internet is a very powerful instrument. Technically, the capacity to recover files at a distance (File retrieval, FTP) is the system's most advanced feature. The possibility of practically unbounded access to data banks and electronically stored text opens the way to the universal diffusion of basic philosophical information. Hypertext and interactive multimedia on CD-ROM are already available, often for free, from the data bases of the major scientific organizations. Educational technologies thus unite with the communications network to form a coherent set of tools, methods and techniques that represents a revolutionary advance in how knowledge, and in our case philosophical knowledge, is organized.

The organization also requires the development of such knowledge resources. We have to learn how to make use of this abundance and availability of information. The issue of the value, not only didactic, but also scientific (and hence, fundamentally, educational, of electronic text is again relevant. There is a question about the real validity of the so-called "ideometric" analysis of such texts. The possibility of storing an almost unlimited amount of text whose main function is to be quantitatively analyzed makes it easy to imagine that this will obviously develop in a rapid and spectacular way. The ease of access to the technology will no doubt have an effect on the kind of work done, and it is not difficult to guess that some researchers will be unable to resist the temptation to produce with minimal effort their own quantitative analyses. Such facility could lead to overspecialization in this area, to more academic competitivity, and an increasing "analyzation", and weakening, of philosophical practice. Once again, the potentiality of a tool of communication could deeply influence the science it is supposed to serve.

The issue of data *retrieval* raises another question: how to get around in Internet maze. Today we are confronted by a surfeit of information that no single individual, however knowledgeable, can manage alone. The major risk here is dispersion. The possibility of connecting at any time to the archives of the United States Supreme Court or the latest newsletter from Oxford can even lead to a sort of "infoneurosis", with total dispersion and concomitant superficiality. Internet can be a terrifying instrument of electronic bombardment, if we use it outside of any context. The possibility of accessing almost *anything* produced on the planet is surely a great step forward, but also a great risk. Anyone who has ever spent entire afternoons browsing through books at random in a library knows the dangers unguided curiosity can hold for the development of solidly organized knowledge. Internet is a powerful tool, and is to be handled with care.

Finally, there is a basic problem. It may happen that the memorization of facts and knowledge will gradually tend to be replaced by skill in manipulating and retrieving large quantities of information, and we should be aware of the danger that this could represent for the humanist conception of culture, which could be radically threatened by this new kind of communication. The hyperspecialization resulting from these new resources could harm the survival of the specific philosophical culture and awareness which alone allow the citizen to become emancipated and to understand our world. The "new ignorance" that the future of Internet could hold would seem to concern both those who are excluded from the world network and those who, on the contrary, are too involved. The danger, as mentioned, is the gradual transformation of the citizen into a *netizen*. If the goal is still to "diffuse philosophy around the world, by forging an unprecedented alliance between culture and the mass media", if technology is to be allied with culture, the fate of civilization in the next millenium will depend on the capacity of mankind to integrate these new tools with our philosophical and civic tradition.

II

SYNERGIES

"Above all, men need to have social relations, to constrain themselves and relate so they can form a unified whole and do all they can to make friendships as strong as possible".

Spinoza, 1665.

To the best of your abilities, do not exclude anything. Do not separate. "Work together" – this is what *syn-ergos* means in Greek – technologies, ideas, people. Their interactions, their cooperations, also part of the word "synergy", always go further than you thought they would, and often contain more surprises than you could imagine.

Let us cease to oppose philosophy and science, concepts and efficiency, books and computers, the mind and modernity, culture and technology, the East and the West, the North and the South... these realities exist, they can be distinct but they are not necessarily antagonistic. They can also be part of innumerable interactions, of unforseen processes of catalysis or precipitation.

It could well be that philosophy, which was said to be destroyed, which we have seen in poor shape, may yet have some great days ahead of it. It could well be that it is "working" with and in democracies, according to ways that are just being invented. It could well be just the beginning. One cannot expect everything of philosophy! It cannot solve – would you believe it? the many new problems faced by men and women today. But its role is far from negligeable.

One of the most singular features of philosophy must be underlined, to conclude: it does not require much knowledge. Already Socrates claimed ignorance. A whole series of philosophers would confirm this form of autonomy of thought with regard to other forms of knowledge. "There are three kinds of government; the republican, the monarchical, the despotic. To discover their nature, it is enough to take the idea that the least educated men have of them", writes, for example, Montesquieu in *L'Esprit des lois.* It is not necessary to know a lot to understand a philosophical argument, or even to invent new ones. Let us stop confusing intelligence and education.

Let us also stop believing that there is an age for philosophy. Almost everything in this survey is about young people. They have priority. But in the responses, there are practically no suggestions concerning adults. After the age of twenty, or twenty five at most, is it the case that metaphysics and moral questions are old topics, that there is nothing left to be solved, that these kinds of interrogations are mere memories of one's youth? Is there a time to rethink the world and another to work in it, without asking questions? If we want philosophy and democracy to continue working together, we must also favour this synergy of generations. We must admit that the right to philosophy should not be barred because of age.

What is inacceptable? Only one thing: the denial of freedom. Anyone who uses freedom to suppress or hinder the freedom of others is in contradiction with the very possibility of human coexistence. Philosophical education must therefore fight against racism and any attempt at the destruction of the unity of mankind. We must avoid confusing freedom with the right to say or do anything. We all know, or should know, that democracy is not licence.

At the end of this journey, what can be done? We can sum up, put the data in order, reflect on the decisions to be taken, discuss priorities, decide about urgencies... This is not the purpose of this small book. A good number of practical proposals have already been mentioned. Others figure in the conclusions to the International Study Days "Philosophy and democracy in the world", reproduced on the following pages. The main issues are the same as the set of responses to the UNESCO questionnaire. If you wish, you can reorganize the information, complete it, communicate about it.

It is not up to me to close this book. It is up to you to conclude.

CONCLUSIONS OF THE INTERNATIONAL STUDY DAYS
"PHILOSOPHY AND DEMOCRACY IN THE WORLD"
(UNESCO document)

On the 15 and 16 February 1995, UNESCO organized International Study Days on the relationship between philosophy and democracy in the world.

Taking part were philosophers from 18 countries, teachers, researchers and university principals belonging to different philosophical schools and traditions.

I – The participants endorsed the initiative taken by the Director-General of UNESCO to encourage international debate about the role of philosophy education in the modern world, about the specific problems raised by such education in the different regions of the world and about the means to be employed to ensure its expansion.

They stressed the importance of the international survey, launched by UNESCO in September 1994, on the situation of philosophy teaching in the world and its place in the cultural life of each country. They pointed out that the survey, which carried on from and extended the first inquiry conducted by UNESCO in 1951, was in keeping with UNESCO's fundamental vocation as an international observatory of the development of knowledge and cultures and as a forum where proposals were made for international action.

The participants noted with satisfaction the rapid progress of the survey and the receipt by UNESCO's Division of Philosophy of replies to the questionnaire from some 60 Member States. They endorsed the decision to put back the deadline for the receipt of replies to 15 April 1995 and expressed the hope that many more States could contribute to that work, which they considered to be of importance.

Taking note of the main themes that had emerged from the replies already analyzed, the participants observed the recent nature of philosophy teaching in many countries and the need to study in greater depth the parallel development of philosophy teaching and democratic processes that could be observed.

The participants stressed that philosophical reflection provided one possible answer to the specialization of teaching, the fragmentation of education and the treatment of study as a means rather than an end.

Among the major themes emerging from the survey, they remarked on the inadequacy of resources for philosophy teaching. They noted the immense needs in terms of human resources, equipment and methods. They felt it necessary that those needs should continue to be inventoried as accurately as possible and that the information thus gathered should be transmitted to the international community.

The participants also emphasized the striking disproportion between the powers attributed to philosophy, such as formation of judgment and the teaching of independence of mind, and the effective means at its disposal. They expressed the hope that the proposals for international action would be directed towards closing that gap.

On the basis of the survey findings relating to the presence of philosophy in cultural life, the participants pointed out that newspapers, magazines, radio and television organizations did not provide sufficient coverage of philosophy. They suggested that new educational methods should be investigated in connection with philosophy education for adults.

II – During these study days, the participants first considered the type of relationship existing between philosophical inquiry and democracy.

In particular, they drew attention to the mistake of believing that philosophy teaching should be used merely to impart moral values or to promote democracy instead of providing an opportunity for giving thought to the basis of those values and to the principles of democratic society.

The participants emphasized the independence of philosophical inquiry and its freedom to criticize political reality of all kinds.

At the same time, they pointed out that the freedom to ask questions and rationally to consider received opinions, which was an integral feature of the practice of philosophy, could be exercised in a democracy and was restricted under other political systems.

They also examined several aspects of the intellectual, political and moral situation that had been created since 1989 by the disappearance of official thinking in those countries which used to espouse Marxism. They emphasized the important role that philosophy teaching could play in those countries in the development of democratic processes.

The statements made by the participants highlighted the main issues specific to philosophy teaching in Asia, Africa, Latin America and the Arab States. They reiterated the need for the different cultures to have a knowledge of each other and drew attention to the fact that philosophical inquiry aspired to universality, while having its roots in particular languages and sociohistorical contexts.

III – Regarding international action on behalf of philosophy education, numerous proposals were put forward by the participants, including:

1. establishment of specialized commissions to prepare philosophy textbooks suited to each of the regions of the world and comparison of philosophy programs and manuals from different countries in order to see where they converge;

2. preparation of regular international exchange programmes, enabling philosophers to describe their work to students from the least-developed countries;

3. planning of a series of expert meetings, one in each region of the world, to examine the specific problems of philosophy teaching and propose solutions adapted to the development of democratic life in each region, following the meeting of specialists to be organized by the National Commission of Korea in August 1995;

4. establishment of UNESCO chairs in philosophy, following the example of what has been planned in Santiago (Chile) (extending to the southern part of South America, in conjunction with the ALPHA program of the European Community) and in Paris (European chair);.

5. study of the detailed philosophy content of human rights teaching and compilation of anthologies of democratic thought;

6. review of the extension of philosophy teaching to secondary education, in association with the countries that have done this in recent years;

7. study and launching of new educational initiatives for the introductory study of philosophical questions by adults, within the framework of continuing education for all;

8. organization of national and international competitions along the lines of philosophy "Olympiads", with the aim of encouraging the practice of philosophical analysis and stimulating, through competition, the interest of young people in philosophy;

9. formulation of proposals for studies on ethics, psychology and the philosophy of religion in the media;

10. study on sex and gender differences in philosophical thinking;

11. support for the organization of international philosophical symposia in Africa;

12. further philosophical study of the principles of democracy;

13. establishment of an international information center for the exchange of philosophy books among institutions in different countries;

14. establishment of an international center for information concerning philosophers suffering persecution.

IV – The participants in the international Study Days "Philosophy and Democracy in the World" call upon UNESCO:

1. **to reaffirm** the importance of philosophy teaching in the education of people, and the need for it to be developed in the various regions of the world, inasmuch as human reason is one;

2. **to continue** the program "Philosophy and Democracy in the World", to publicize the results of the survey and prepare follow-up action to it;

3. **to take** new initiatives to enable philosophers to participate in the study and discussion of the main questions affecting mankind today;

4. **to encourage** methods of teaching philosophy that involve the use both of books, distance education (in collaboration with UNESCO chairs in philosophy), audio-visual material and information technology;

5. **to give** support to work in comparative philosophy with the aim of arriving at a fuller understanding of the areas where the philosophical thinking of different cultures converges or diverges;

6. **to encourage** the establishment of societies of philosophy teachers in all countries;

7. **to facilitate** access by the philosophical institutions of the less favoured countries to the worldwide electronic networks.

At the conclusion of their work, the participants in the International Study Days "Philosophy and Democracy in the World" adopted the Paris Declaration for Philosophy, included at the beginning of this book, with a list of participants. Those of you who wish to add your name to the Paris Declaration for Philosophy, *or to receive the newsletter summarizing the activities of the Division of Philosophy, or to send us your comments and suggestions concerning this book , please write to:*

"Philosophy and democracy in the world"
UNESCO Division of philosophy
1, rue Miollis,
75732 Paris Cedex 15

SUMMARY TABLE

This summary table does not claim to be scientifically rigorous.

In the case of some of the questions, the Member States did not always have available figures.

The data is therefore an estimation, and should be used cautiously.

However, it seemed useful to put together these general indications.

The first column indicates the period of the last important reform in philosophy teaching.

The " - " indicates no answer.

The words "non significant" indicate that the question does not apply.

COUNTRIES (Classification by region)	Period of establishment of the present system	Where philosophy is taught	Estimated percent of philosophy students (on total number of students)	Estimated percent of students attending philosophy classes	Overall attention given to philosophy
Benin	1960 s	Secondary	5 to 14 %	60 %	Increasing
Cameroon	1950 s	Secondary	5 to 10 %	Not significant	Stable
Cape Verde	–	Secondary	No university	No university	Not significant
Chad	1960 s	Secondary	2 to 3 %	Not significant	Increasing
Cote d'Ivoire	1960 s	Secondary	4 to 5 %	Not significant	Increasing
Liberia	1968	Higher	Not significant	Not significant	Increasing
Malawi	1966	Higher	7,5 %	–	Increasing
Mali	1960 s	Secondary	25 %	Not significant	Stable
Nigeria	1966	Higher	3 to 5 %	100 %	Increasing
Senegal	1930 s	Secondary	2 %	–	Increasing
Zaire	1960 s	Secondary	7 %	95 %	Increasing
Iran (Islamic Republic of)	–	Higher	–	30 %	Increasing
Jordan	1960 s	Higher	2 to 3 %	100 %	Stable
Kuwait	1960 s	Secondary	0,08 %	–	Increasing
Lebanon	1946	Secondary	1 to 2 %	70 %	Stable
Mauritania	1983	Secondary	3 %	0 %	Stable
Morocco	1950 s	Secondary	0,78 %	0 %	Stable
Qatar	–	Higher	Not significant	Not significant	Increasing
Syrian Arab Republic	1925	Secondary	–	–	Increasing
Tunisia	1957	Secondary	2,45 %	–	Increasing

Australia	–	Higher	5 %	Not significant	Stable
China	1950 s	Secondary	–	100 % (theorical)	Increasing
Democratic People's Republic of Korea	1946	Secondary	1 %	around 70 %	Increasing
Indonesia	–	Higher	1,2 %	20 %	Stable
Pakistan	1952	Higher	1 %	Not significant	Increasing
Russian Federation	1950 s	Higher	0,6 %	100 % (theorical)	Not significant
Thailand	1947	Higher	2 to 3 %	100 %	Stable
Albania	1992	Secondary	0,3 %	5 to 10 %	Increasing
Belarus	1991	Higher	–	100 %	Increasing
Bulgaria	1990	Secondary	2 to 3 %	30 %	Increasing
Croatia	–	Secondary	0,5 %	30 %	Increasing
Czech Republic	1989	Secondary	–	–	Increasing
Finland		Secondary	–	–	Increasing
France	1844-1925	Secondary	1 %	–	Increasing
Greece	–	Secondary	0,5 to 1 %	30 %	Increasing
Hungary	1989	Secondary	–	40 to 50 %	Increasing
Italy	1853-1923	Secondary	10 %	Not significant	Increasing
Luxemburg	1968	Secondary	Less than 10 %	10 %	Stable
Malta	–	Higher	–	–	Increasing
Norway	1811	Higher	1 %	100 %	Increasing
Netherlands	1990	Secondary	1 to 7 %	20 %	Increasing
Portugal	1974	Secondary	1 %	Not signidicant	Increasing
Romania	1920 s	Secondary	2 %	80 %	Increasing
San Marino	1983	Secondary	–	20 %	Increasing
Slovakia	–	Secondary	–	100 %	Increasing
Slovenia	–	Secondary	–	50 %	Increasing
Turkey	1930 s	Secondary	0,25 %	–	Increasing
United Kingdom	Mddle Ages	Higher	10 % (Oxford)	Not signidicant	Stable
United States of America	Not significant	Higher	1 to 3 %	around 50 %	Increasing
Argentina	1985	Secondary	5 to 6 %	–	Increasing
Brazil	1971	Secondary-	–	5 to 10 %	Increasing
Chile	1890 s	Secondary	1 %	25 %	Increasing
Colombia	1960 s	Secondary	2 to 5 %	–	Stable
Cuba	1960 s	Higher	–	100 %	Stable
Dominican Republic	1950	Secondary	–	100 %	Increasing
Honduras	1978	Higher	0,1 %	100 %	Increasing
Nicaragua	1990	Secondary	–	Not signidicant	Increasing
Uruguay	1945	Secondary	–	–	Increasing
Venezuela	–	Secondary	0,1 %	25 %	Increasing

ACKNOWLEDGMENTS

We present our sincere apologies to any person whose name, by mistake, has been omitted or mispelled. All due corrections will be made in the next edition.

Gratitude and thanks are extended, firstly, to all the people for the time and energy spent in answering the many questions of this survey, and to those who have transmitted the documents throughout the world.
Answers came to UNESCO in five different ways, and the following lists are organized according to this distinction.
Our special thanks to the UNESCO's National Commissions for their unique contribution to the survey, to the Permanent Delegations of Members States for their constant support to the project, to the Ministries of Education, to Philosophical institutions and to those who responded on an individual basis.

The following abbreviations are used: Dept. = Department; Dir. = Director; S. g. = Secretary-General; P.D. = Permanent Delegate; Nat. = National; Phi. = Philosophy; F.S. = First Secretary; Prof. = Professor; Univ. = University.

RESPONSES TRANSMITTED BY UNESCO'S NATIONAL COMMISSIONS

Benin (S. g.: Mr Mouhamed Jacquet [interim]).
Answers compiled by: Prof. Gervais Kissezounon (Porto Novo), Prof. Coovi Paul Abitan (Porto Novo) with the participation of Prof. François Dossou (Cotonou).

Cameroon (S. g.: Mr Robert Mbelle Mbappe).
Answers compiled by: Prof. Marcien Towa, Prof. Simon Menye Ngono (Bafia), Prof. Ngoa Mebada, Prof. Simon Pierre Amougui, Prof. Michel Ngueti, Prof. Hubert Mono Ndjana (Univ. of Yaounde I), Dr Pierre-Paul Okah-Atenga (Univ. of Yaounde I).

Cape Verde (S. g.: Ms. Fatima Carvalho).
Answers compiled by: Prof. Isidoro Tavares (Achada Santo Antonio Lyceum).

Chad (S. g.: Djibrine Hisseine Kreinki.
Answers compiled by: Ministry of Education (Univ. of N'Djamena, faculty of literature and social sciences, Dpt. of philosophy).

Colombia (S. g.: Ms. Natalia Martin-Leyes B.).

Answers compiled by: Dr Gerardo Andrade Gonzalez (Univ. del Cauca), Ministry of National Education, Prof. Silvio Herrera Herrera, National Inspector (Santafe de Bogotá).

Cote d'Ivoire (S. g.: Ms. Anna Manouan).

Answers compiled by: Prof. Tanella Boni-Kone. (Univ. of Abidjan).

Croatia (S. g.: Mr Dilo Milinovic).

Answers compiled by: Institute of Phi. (Univ. of Zagreb).

Denmark (S. g.: Ms. Hanne Rosendahl Jensen).

Answers compiled by: Prof. Finn Collin (Dept of Phil, Univ. of Copenhagen).

France (S. g.: Mr Georges Poussin).

Answers compiled by: Prof. Marcel Lucien, Doyen of the Inspection Générale of Philosophy, Prof. Christiane Chauvire (Univ. of Nantes), Prof. Jean-Michel Vienne (Univ. of Nantes), Prof. Anne Lewis-Loubignac, consultant with the French Commission for UNESCO.

Guyana (S. g.: Ms. Carmen E. Jarvis).

Answers compiled by: Prof. A.M.B. Sankies, Deputy-Vice-Chancellor (Faculty of Arts).

Indonesia (S. g.: Mr W.P. Napitupulu).

Answers compiled by: Executive Board of Higher Education, Ministry of Education and Culture.

Iran (Islamic Republic of) (S. g.: Dr A. Zargar).

Answers compiled by: Univ. of Ispahan.

Jordan (S. g.: Ms. Janette Bermamet).

Answers compiled by: Prof. Hasan 'Alâ ad-Dîn, Director-General of Cultural and Public Relations and Education Information, Ministry of Education.

Kuwait (S. g.: Mr Sulaiman Al Onaizi).

Answers compiled by: Dept of Phi. (Univ. of Kuwait).

Lebanon (S. g.: Mr Hisham Nashabe).

Answers compiled by: Centre de recherche et du développement pédagogique.

Luxembourg (S. g.: Mr Turpel).

Answers compiled by: Prof. Jean-Paul Harpes and Prof. J.-P. Roger Strainchamps.

Malawi (S. g.: Mr C.H. Longwe [interim]).

Answers compiled by: Dr Hermes F. Chidammodzi (Dir. Dept. of Phil., Univ. of Malawi).

Mali (S. g.: Ms. Aminata Sall).

Answers compiled by: Prof. Abdoul Kader Samake, Prof. Ibrahim Sagaya Toure (E.N.S. of Bamako), Prof. Yaya Sissouma, Chief Inspector of Philosophy, Prof. Yamoussa Kanta.

Malta (S. g.: Mr J.G. Agius).

Answers compiled by: Social Science Section of the Education Dept.

Mauritania (S. g. Mr Ahmed Beddy Ould Ahmedou Vall).

Answers compiled by: Prof. Mohamed Mahmoud Ould El Hadjbrahim, Chief Inspector of secondary and technical education, Prof. Sy Tahirou, Inspector of Philosophy, Prof. Mohamed Vall Ould Cheikh, Inspector of French language education.

Netherlands (S. g.: Mr Dick Lageweg).

Answers compiled by: Vereniging voor Filosofie onderwijs, Drs M. Walenkamp.

Nicaragua (S. g.: Ms. Claudia Valle).

Answers compiled by: Prof. Juan Bosco Cuadra (Ministry of Education).

Nigeria (S. g.: Mr Y.M.O. Nwafor).

Answers compiled by: Prof. Godwin Sogolo (Univ. of Ibadan), Dr S. Iniobong Udoidem. (Univ. of Port Harcourt).

Norway (S. g.: Ms. Mari Hareide).

Answers compiled by: Prof. Per Ariensen, Prof. Kolbein Brede, Prof. Arild Pedersen, Prof. Astrid Lied, Prof. Oystein Skar. (Dept of Phi., Univ. of Oslo).

Qatar (Ass. S. g.: Prof. Abdul Rahman M. Ali).

Answers compiled by: Univ. of Qatar.

Republic of Korea (S. g.: Mr In-Suk Cha).

Answers compiled by: Dr Kyung-Sig Hwang (Dept of Phi., Nat. Univ. of Seoul).

Russian Federation (S. g.: Mr Alexei D. Joukov).

Answers compiled by: Prof. Ruben Grantovich Apresyan (Institute of Phi., Moscow).

Saint-Marin (S. g.: Ms. Antonella Benedettini).

Answers compiled by: (not mentioned).

Senegal (S. g.: Mr Assane Hane).

Answers compiled by: Prof. Babou Sene, Chief Inspector of Philosophy, École Normale Supérieure of Dakar.

Slovakia (S. g.: Mr Miroslav Musil).

Answers compiled by: Dept of Ethics and Political Studies, Univ. Comenius (Bratislava).

Slovenia (S. g.: Mr Zofija Klemen-Krek).

Answers compiled by: Prof. Marjan Simenc (Pedagogical Institute, Ljubljania), Dr Janez Juhant (Dean, Univ. of Ljubljania).

Switzerland (S. g.: M.B. Theurillat).

Answers compiled by: (not mentioned).

Syrian Arab Republic (S. g.: Mr Hassam Al-Hamoui).

Answers compiled by: Ministry of Education.

Thailand (S. g.: Dr Surat Silpa-Anan).

Answers compiled by: Ministry of Education, Dept of Teacher Education.

Tunisia (S. g.: Mr Zeineb Haaouia).

Answers compiled by: Prof. Fathi Triki (Dean, Univ. of Sfax), Prof. Ali Channoufi, Prof. Taoufiq Cherif, Prof. Mohammed Mahjoub, Prof. Hmaied Ben Aziza, Prof. Omran Boukhari, Prof. Najib Abdelmoula.

Zaire (S. g.: Mr Ikepe Ebale Belotsi).

Answers compiled under the supervision of Prof. Biangany Gomanu Tamp'no, Director-General of the University Institute of Social Sciences, Economics, Philosophy and Arts (ISPL) and President of the Board of Administration of CEPOD (Centre d'Etudes Politiques et de formation à la Démocratie) and of the CCAM in collaboration with Prof. Mambu Luenga Mamana, Prof. Pelenga Kia Mbuila, Prof. Mavinga Tsafunenga, Prof. Balon Ituni Bombane, Prof. Abe Pangulu, Prof. Mutombo Elikya, Prof. Betu Mulumba, Prof. Nsusanzo Ben-Amar Nekes, Prof. Balingate Nlata.

ANSWERS GIVEN BY THE PERMANENT DELEGATIONS OF MEMBER STATES

Argentina (P.D.: Mr Leopoldo Torres-Aguero).

Answers compiled by: Prof. Susana Villavicencio (Buenos Aires).

Australia (P.D.: Mr Jonathan Brown).

Answers compiled by: Prof. John Bigelow, Dept of Phi., Monash University.

Belarus (F.S.: E. Ioukevitch).

Answers compiled by: Prof. T.A. Gorolevitch, Prof. S.I. Sanko, Prof. Lukashevich V.K., Prof. T.M. Touzowa (Law and Philosophy Institute, Science Academy of Belarus).

Chile (P.D.: Mr Jorge Edwards).

Answers compiled by: Chilian Academy of Social, Political and Moral Sciences of the Institute of Chili.

China (S. g.: Mr Li Jiangang, Affaires SHS).

Answers compiled by: Institute of Philosophical Research of the Chinese Academy of Social Sciences.

Italy (P.D.: Mr Giancarlo Leo).
Answers compiled by: Ministry of Public Education.

Pakistan (P.D.: Dr R.A. Siyal).

Answers compiled by: Univ. of Karachi, Dr Muhammad Amin (Bahauddin Zakariya Univ., Multan) and Univ. of Sindh (Jamshoro).

Portugal (P.D.: Mr José Antonio Moya Ribera).

Answers compiled by: Ministry of Education, Department of Secondary Education, Faculty of Arts of Lisbon.

Turkey (interim: Mr Taner Karakas).

Answers compiled by: Prof. Ioanna Kuçuradi, Secretary-General of the International Federation of Philosophical Societies (FISP), Hacettepe Univ., Dept of Phi. (Ankara).

Uganda (P.D.: Mr E.B. Kawesa).

RESPONSES SENT BY THE MINISTRIES OF NATIONAL EDUCATION

Brazil

Answers compiled by: Prof. Sergio Nicolaiewsky (Vice-Director, State Univ. of Rio Grande do Sul), Prof. José Celso Aquino Marques (Collège d'application), Prof. Gilberto Kmohan (Technical School of Commerce), Prof. Fernando Fleck (Dept of Phi.), Prof. Agnaldo Portugal, Prof. Lucia Helena C. Zabotto Pulino, Prof. Dr Wilton Barroso (Univ. of Brasilia).

Dominican Republic

Answers compiled by: Ms. Prof. Jacqueline Malagon (Secretaria de Estado de Educación, Bellas Artes y Cultos, División de Planificación educativa).

Finland (Ministry of National Education, Cultural Affairs Secretary: Prof. Eeva Hippula).

Answers compiled by: Prof. Pekka Elo and Prof. Mikko Yrjonsuuri (Dept of Phi., Univ. of Joensuu).

Greece (Dir. of Dept: Mr Fr Meropouli).

Answers compiled by: Dr Christos Terezis (Univ. of Patras), Aspasia Papadopoulou.

Honduras (Dir-in-Chief of Planification: Ms. Josefina Gamero Pinel)

Answers compiled by: Prof. Oscar Soriano (Dept of Phi., Nat. Univ. of Honduras), Prof. Claudia Yolanda Mejia Galo (Dir-in-Chief of the Ministry of Public Education), Prof. Renan Rapalo (Dept of Phi., Nat. Univ. of Honduras).

Uruguay (Prof. Carlos Zubillaga, Facultad de Humanidades y Ciencias de la Educación, Montevideo).

Answers compiled by: Prof. Carlos Caorsi, Prof. Miguel Andreoli, Prof. Mario Otero (Institute of Phi. Commission).

PHILOSOPHICAL INSTITUTIONS AND MISCELLANEOUS

Colombia

Colegio Mayor de Nuestra Señora del Rosario (Bogotá).

Cuba

Orcal, Regional office for Culture in Latin America and in the Caribbean Islands: Dr Hernán Crespo Toral.

Answers compiled by: Dr Pablo Guadarrama Gonzalez (Univ. of Santa Clara); Cuban Society of Philosophical Research (Invest, Ong), Dr Norma Galvez Periut, Dr Dora Jorge Farinas, Dr Magaly Rodriguez Gonzalez, Lic. Lissette Mendoza Portales, Lic. Cecilia Galvez Henry, Lic. Maria Concepción Gonzalez Basanta, Lic. Graciela Montero Cepero (Institut supérieur pédagogique 'Enrique José Varona'), Prof. Aurelio Alonso (Centre for Latin American studies (CEA, Ong), Dr Juan Mari Lois ('Felix Varela' Centre, Ong).

Malta

Univ. of Malta, Msida-Malta, Faculty of Arts, Dept of Philosophy. Ms. Mary Ann Cassar, Rev. Prof. Peter Serracino

Inglott (Director of Education, Univ. of Malta), Prof. Joe Friggieri (Assist.-Director).

Venezuela

Instituto Internacional de Estudios Avanzados, Unidad de Filosofía IDEA (Caracas), Mr Ernesto Mayz Vallenilla.

Answers compiled by: Prof. M. Ayala, Prof. G. Sarmiento, Prof. A. Vallota.

INDIVIDUAL RESPONSES

Albania Prof. Zija Xholi (Univ. of Tirana), Prof. Artan Fuga (Univ. of Tirana), Prof. Aleksander Kocani (Univ. of Tirana).

Argentina Prof. Horacio Gonzalez (Univ. of Rosario), Prof. Liliana Herrero (Univ. of Buenos Aires), Inés Dussel (Flacso), Prof. Graciela Frigerio (Buenos Aires).

Belgium Prof. Jacques Etienne (Catholic Univ. of Louvain)

Bulgaria Prof. Ivan G. Kolev (Univ. of Sofia), Prof. Tzotcho Boyadjiev (Univ. St. Clement of Ohrid, Sofia), Dr Christo Todorov (Univ. of Sofia).

Canada Prof. Jack Iwanicki (Univ. of New Brunswick).

Chile Prof. Ezequiel de Alaso, Prof. María Cecilia Sanchez (Univ. of Talca), Prof. José Jara (Univ. de Valparaiso), Prof. Marcos García de la Huerta (Univ. of Chile, Santiago).

Colombia Prof. Victor Florian (Dept of Phi., National Univ. of Colombia, Bogotá), Prof. Bernardo Correa Lopez (Dir. Dept Phi., Univ. Nat. of Colombie, Bogota.

Czech Republic Prof. Petr Horak (Univ. of Mazaryk, Arts Faculty – Dept of Phi., Brno, through the intermediary of Prof. Jana Sturzova (Faculty of Phi., Prague), Ms. Prof. Peskova, Ms. Sclegelova (PhD).

France Prof. Christine Chevret (Lyon), Prof. Catherine Clément (Vienne, Autriche).

Germany Prof. Ulrich Johannes Schneider (Univ. of Leipzig).

Hong Kong Prof. A.K.C. Nem (Dept of Phi., Hong Kong University).

Hungary Prof. Szabo (Teacher's training college of Kaposvar).

Liberia Prof. Wolor Topor (Univ. of Liberia, Monrovia).

Morocco Prof. Ben Omar Boubker (Dept of Phi, Univ. of Rabat) and Prof. Kabbaj Mohammed Mustapha (Ministry of Cultural Affairs, Rabat).

Nigeria Prof. Raphael A. Akanmidu (Univ. of Ilorin).

Romania Prof. Corneliu Mircea (Timisoara), Prof. Georges G. Contandache (Bucarest), Prof. Rodica Croitoru (Bucarest), Prof. Petru Ioan.

Russian Federation Prof. A.L. Dobrokhotov (Faculty of Phi., State Univ. of Moscow), Prof. M.V. Lomonossov (Univ. of Moscow).

Tunisia Ms. Prof. Melika Ouelbani (Univ. of Tunis I).

United Kingdom of Great-Britain and Northern Ireland Prof. Michael Dummett (Oxford).

Unites States of America Prof. Richard Rorty (Univ. of Virginia), Prof. Richard Shusterman (Dept of Phi., Temple Univ., Philadelphia), Prof. Tyler Burge (Dept of Phi., UCLA).

Uruguay Prof. Mauricio Langon, Inspector of philosophy education in secondary schools (Solymar).

Yugoslavia Prof. Rada Ivekovic.

This book owes a great deal to research papers written for UNESCO for the "Philosophy and Democracy in the world" programme, extracts of which are presented in this volume. Unabridged versions of these papers have been published and are available.

"Processus démocratiques et enseignement philosophique en Afrique" (Paulin J. Hountondji, National University of Benin);

"Philosophie et démocratie au Chili" (Maria Cecilia Sanchez, University of Talca);

"La situation de la philosophie dans l'ancienne Europe socialiste" (Stéphane Douailler, University of Paris VIII);

"La situation de la philosophie en Allemagne après 1990" (Ulrich Johannes Schneider, University of Leipzig);

"Philosophie et démocratie en Amérique du Nord : problèmes et perspectives" (Christian Delacampagne, Boston);

"La question du philosophe et du citoyen dans l'évolution des régimes politiques en Amérique Latine" (Patrice Vermeren, Centre d'Études Politiques de la Sorbonne);

"Interdépendance économique, démocratisation et philosophie" (François Rachline, Institut d'Études Politiques, Paris);

"Techniques électroniques et pédagogie philosophique" (Luca M. Scarantino);

"Enseignement scientifique et enseignement philosophique" (Dominique Lecourt, University of Paris VII);

"Évolution de la philosophie politique et la place du citoyen" (Étienne Tassin, University of Paris VIII).

I would also like to extend my gratitude to those who have helped and advised me at one moment or another during this work:

• Mr Jean d'Ormesson, President of the International Council for Philosophy and Social Sciences (CIPSh, Ong), and Mr Ehsane Naraghi, consultant at UNESCO, both of whom supported the original project of the present book.

• Mohammed Allal Sinaceur, former director of the Philosophy Division at UNESCO, for his precious advice.

• Mr Serguei Lazarev, currently in charge of the Section for Tolerance, for his guidance;

• Ms. Ayyam Sureau, in charge of the "Rencontres Philosophiques de l'UNESCO";

• Ms. Ioanna Kuçuradi, Secretary-General of the Fédération Internationale des Sociétés de Philosophie, who kindly published the questionnaire in the FISP bulletin and gave an account of the conference held on February 15 and 16, 1995;

• Mr Jacques Havet, formerly in charge of Philosophy and Social Sciences at the UNESCO;

• Mr François Jullien, Professor of Chinese literature and Civilization at the University of Paris VII;

• Ms. Catherine Clément, philosopher and novelist;
• Mr Christian Delacampagne, French cultural attaché in Boston (USA).

Heartfelt thanks to the following people of the Philosophy Division of UNESCO for collaborating with such energy on this project:
• Mr Daniel Janicot, Vice-Director-in-chief of the Executive Board of the UNESCO, who continually supported the activities of this Division placed under his responsability and has paid particular attention as to the realization of this project.
• Mrs Renée Lugassy, who, up until June 1995, was in charge of the secretariat of the "Philosophy and Democracy in the world" programme, and who was responsible for organizing the dispatch of questionnaires and the international meeting held in February 1995.
• Mr Patrice Vermeren, researcher at the Centre d'Études Politiques of the Sorbonne, who, thanks to the board of Directors of the Centre National de Recherche Scientifique, has been able to work, since January 1995, with the Philosophy Division of the UNESCO.
• Mrs. Marie-Ange Théobald, in charge of the Newsletter of the Philosophy Division and of extra-budgetary resources.
• Miss Véronique Aldebert, secretary of the Philosophy Division.
• Miss Anne-Cécile Aria and Ms. Jutta von Reitzenstein, both of whom have contributed in a precious way to this survey during their training periods within the Philosophy Division.

Very special thanks to those who, by their accuracy and speed of work, have made the existence of this book possible and in such short time:
• Miss Murielle Ohnona-Weizman, responsible for the thematical analysis of answers.
• Mrs. Yvette Gogue, who has processed numerous data and revised the manuscript.
• Mrs Catherine Cullen, responsible for the English version.

I would also like to thank Ms. Ihsane Elamounni for her well-advised help. The patience and tenderness of Marie Droit, my daughter, and of Tatiana and Laura Atran-Fresco, her friends, are not subject to acknowledgments. But they have helped me, the three of them, tremendously.

Finally, I insist on stressing the fact that without the trusting will of Federico Mayor, Director-General of the UNESCO, nothing would have been possible. May these words be a token of my gratitude.

Roger-Pol DROIT

Born in 1949, Roger-Pol Droit is a former student of the École Normale Supérieure of Saint-Cloud and has an *agrégation* in philosophy (1972). Columnist at the newspaper *Le Monde*, he is also a researcher at the Centre National de la Recherche Scientifique (philosophy).

He taught philosophy from 1979 to 1989.

His research work deals with the interpretations of Indian doctrines, particularly Buddhism, by European philosophers. He has published a number of studies on this subject in specialized journals as well as his first book entitled *L'Oubli de l'Inde. Une amnésie philosophique* (PUF 1989, new edition: Le Livre de Poche, 1992). He is currently working on *Le Culte du Néant. Philosophie et bouddhisme*, to be published by les Éditions du Seuil.

As a journalist of *Le Monde* for the past twenty years he has reviewed hundreds of books on philosophy and has published interviews of Michel Foucault, Paul Ricœur, Emmanuel Lévinas, Jurgen Habermas, Claude Lévi-Strauss, and Umberto Eco, among others.

From 1989 to 1995, Roger-Pol Droit established and presented the *Le Monde*-Le Mans forum involving up to 200 participants. Le Monde-Editions has published six volumes of texts that he compiled and edited: *Science et philosophie pour quoi faire?* (1990), *Les Grecs, les Romains et nous. L'Antiquité est-elle moderne ?* (1991), *Comment penser l'argent?* (1992), *L'Art est-il une connaissance ?* (1993), *Où est le bonheur ?* (1994, *L'Avenir aujourd'hui. Dépend-il de nous ?* (1995).

In November 1994, Roger-Pol Droit became Philosophy adviser to the Director-General of UNESCO.

IMPRIMÉ EN FRANCE PAR BRODARD ET TAUPIN
2475C-5 - Usine de La Flèche le 15-09-1995
Dépôt légal : septembre 1995
ISBN : 923 - 103207 - 0